Leadership: The Art of Delegation

The Sunday Times 'Business Skills' series currently comprises books on total quality, management, personal skills and leadership skills.

This first class series has received a warm welcome from readers and critics alike: the opinion of Christopher Lorenz of the *Financial Times*, for example, is that it is 'excellent . . . well worth reading'. It is designed to build into an essential management library of authoritative and handsomely produced books. Each one, providing a definitive standalone summary of best business theory and practice in its field, is also carefully co-ordinated to complement *The Sunday Times* 'Business Skills' video training package of the same name produced by Taylor Made Films.

BOOKS IN THE SERIES:

QUALITY: MEASURING AND MONITORING
Tony Bendell, John Kelly, Ted Merry, Fraser Sims
ISBN 0-7126-5514-X (P)

QUALITY: TOTAL CUSTOMER SERVICE
Lynda King Taylor
ISBN 0-7126-9843-4

QUALITY: SUSTAINING CUSTOMER SERVICE
Lynda King Taylor
ISBN 0-7126-5519-0 (P)

QUALITY: ACHIEVING EXCELLENCE
Edgar Wille
ISBN 0-7126-9863-9

QUALITY: CHANGE THROUGH TEAMWORK
Rani Chaudhry-Lawton, Richard Lawton, Karen Murphy,
Angela Terry
ISBN 0-7126-9833-7

EFFECTIVE MEETINGS
Phil Hodgson, Jane Hodgson
ISBN 0-7126-9873-6

TIME MANAGEMENT
Martin Scott
ISBN 0-7126-9853-1

SUCCESSFUL PRESENTATIONS
Carole McKenzie
ISBN 0-7126-5691-X (P)

LEADERSHIP: THE ART OF MOTIVATION
Nick Thornely and Dan Lees
ISBN 0-7126 5646-4 (P)

Leadership: The Art of Delegation

by

David Oates

CENTURY
BUSINESS

Copyright © David Oates 1993

The right of David Oates to be identified as the author of this
work has been asserted by him in accordance with the Copyright, Designs and
Patents Acts, 1988

First published in Great Britain 1993
by Century Business
An imprint of Random House UK Limited
20 Vauxhall Bridge Road, London SW1V 2SA

Random House Australia (Pty) Limited
20 Alfred Street, Milsons Point
Sydney, NSW 2061, Australia

Random House New Zealand Limited
18 Poland Road, Glenfield
Auckland 10, New Zealand

Random House South Africa (Pty) Limited
PO Box 337, Bergvlei, South Africa

Set in Bembo by SX Composing Ltd, Rayleigh, Essex
Printed and bound in Great Britain by Mackays of Chatham PLC, Kent

British Library Cataloguing in Publication Data
A catalogue record for this book is available from the British Library.

ISBN 0-7126-5651-0

Contents

Acknowledgements		vii
1	DEFINING DELEGATION	1
2	WHY DELEGATE?	5
3	THE CLIMATE FOR DELEGATION – NEW INFLUENCES	28
4	EMPOWERMENT	57
5	THE DELEGATION PROCESS	87
6	PERFORMANCE COACHING	108
7	DELEGATING TO THE RIGHT PERSON	117
8	FEEDBACK	133
9	DELEGATING IN FOUNDER-MANAGED SMALL FIRMS	143
10	DELEGATING TO TEAMS	148
	(a) Toshiba	152
	(b) Sherwood Computer Services	157
	(c) Digital Equipment	165
	(d) Rank Xerox	168
11	THE PACE SETTERS	172
	(a) Rank Xerox	173
	(b) Hewlett-Packard	191
	(c) W.H. Smith	198
	(d) Cow & Gate	206
	(e) BP	219
Bibliography		233
Index		234

To my wife, Johanna,
who allowed me to delegate to her some of the
tasks that made this book possible.

Acknowledgements

Authorship is a lonely occupation and one that does not lend itself to a lot of delegation. But the finished product is the sum total of an enormous amount of wisdom, knowledge and experience from a host of different people. It is only the willingness of so many people to part with so much information that makes a book of this kind possible.

I am especially grateful to two people – Jim Durcan of Ashridge Management College and Adrian Savage of Assessment Design Services. Their overview of the latest thinking about delegation and empowerment techniques helped in no small measure to provide the framework on which this book was built. Numerous other people helped to put flesh on the skeleton. They include: Warren Bennis; Fiona McLaren (Speechly Bircham); Barry Curnow; Alex Bruce (Texaco); Dr Barry Brown (The Independent Assessment & Research Centre); Stephen Taylor (Kinsley Lord); John Garnett; Michael Thomas (PA Consulting Group); Bob Dixon (The Industrial Society); Prof. Bernard Taylor, Tony Knight, Sheila Rothwell and Ann Todd (Henley Management College); Michael Stanton, Dr Paul Taffinder and David Taylor (Coopers Deloitte).

In addition, I owe a debt of gratitude to a number of leading edge companies that were kind enough to spare the time to explain how they are applying academic theory in practice: Toshiba Consumer Products (George Harris); Sherwood Computer Services (Bob Thomas); Digital Equipment Co. (Chris Lever, Phil Scott and Alastair Wright); Rank Xerox (UK) Ltd (Vernon Zelmer and Shaun Pantling); BP (Roy Williams); Hewlett-Packard (Mike Haffenden and David Marchant); Cow & Gate (Peter Roebuck, Linda Chick and Neil Coxon).

1. Defining Delegation

The most widely accepted definition of a manager is someone who gets things done through other people. That is what management is all about. It is the ability to delegate that distinguishes the good manager from the bad. The manager who utilises the skills, aptitudes and commitment of his subordinates to develop them and broaden their experience is the one most likely to succeed and become a prime candidate for promotion.

But delegation is a much misunderstood technique and one that is undergoing considerable review in the light of sweeping changes in the way organizations are being run. The principles, however, remain the same and in order to understand the benefits of delegation it is important to grasp the significance of three terms that are frequently mentioned in this book – responsibility, authority and accountability.

Responsibility relates to the ownership of the task that has been delegated. As soon as a subordinate is entrusted with a project it is his or her responsibility to see it completed in accordance with the aims and deadlines agreed with the delegating manager. The subordinate may require support and coaching, but the responsibility to see the job through has been passed down the line like the baton in a relay race.

The authority is the power that is invested in the subordinate to enable the responsibility to be successfully discharged. This means ensuring that the subordinate is authorised to use whatever resources are necessary to perform the delegated task and that he or she is in a position to make the necessary decisions relating to it. Nevertheless, senior managers are always accountable for what happens in their sector of the organisation. Simply because they have passed on responsibility and authority to the subordinate does not mean that they can abdicate all accountability when something goes wrong.

It is this risk element that causes many senior managers to be reluctant delegators. They are only too aware that the buck will always stop with them and yet they feel that they have lost control once they have handed over a task to a subordinate.

The philosophical way of looking at it is that there is a degree of risk in all innovative management and that the benefits of delegating well outweigh the dangers involved. The advantages and drawbacks of delegating are explored in the next chapter.

The whole issue of authority and accountability is coming under review as a result of the trend towards empowerment, a very fashionable buzz word in management circles these days. Empowerment, where delegation is concerned, essentially means enabling employees to take personal initiatives beyond the scope of their normal work but within a set of established company values. It promises to have a powerful impact on the way devolved responsibility is handled in organisations and this is looked at in some depth in Chapter 4.

One of the reasons empowerment's time has come is that many organisations are making radical changes to their corporate structures. The pyramid is becoming flattened as companies de-layer their organisations by cutting out huge swathes of middle management in the drive to become leaner and more competitive. Many of the functions that middle managers used to fulfil are fast disappearing. There are no longer enough of them around to provide the kind of supervisory support that was once their prime role. Inevitably, this requires responsibility to be pushed further down the line and decisions to be made closer to the coalface. Unless subordinates are empowered to take initiatives corporate life could easily grind to a halt.

But it is not just the flattening of the pyramid that is having a profound impact on methods of delegation. There are a host of other influences that are making the old hierarchical system of passing instructions down the line an impracticality. Globalisation, networking and teleworking are all causing delegation to be looked at anew. The trend towards internationalisation makes it very difficult to retain control at the centre. Similarly, informal networks that span the globe, bypassing official reporting lines, reject the old-style command structures. Teleworking, by its very nature, undermines traditional methods of supervision. How can a supervisor check the work of a subordinate who works from home and is invisible for the most part?

All these developments are raising profound issues about the best way to delegate so that control does not give way to anarchy. There are still a lot of unanswered questions. But one view that seems to prevail is that if delegation is done for the right reasons it can be a powerful and enriching tool that benefits manager and subordinate alike. If the intention is simply to pass on unwanted tasks, the true benefits of delegation will be wasted. The more enlightened approach is that delegation should be used to enrich the jobs of subordinates by stretching them and broadening their experience. In this way they will grow in the job and help facilitate effective succession planning. A fully developed subordinate is ripe for promotion. Such subordinates are also likely to be more committed and motivated.

Taking this argument a stage further, the idea is growing that delegation can be used as a tool for performance coaching. The benefits are that performance coaching is an ongoing daily activity which makes use of existing resources and builds on existing working relationships. By contrast, external training courses are expensive, time-consuming and often of short-term impact.

Performance coaching is also growing in importance for other reasons. As responsibility is increasingly devolved to those employees closest to the customer, the role of senior managers is radically changing in a number of leading companies, some of which are profiled in the final chapters of this book. Instead of performing a command and control role, they are acting as coaches and counsellors to front-line staff. Indeed, some of these pioneering companies have even inverted the traditional pyramid organisation structure to facilitate this fundamental change of approach.

Such companies are trail-blazing new management styles that

may well provide a model for the future. In the meantime, however, the majority are still operating along more traditional lines, which require a more orthodox approach to delegation.

At some stage in his career, every senior manager is going to have to delegate. Often executives are forced to delegate as the result of a crisis. They have to make an urgent unscheduled overseas business trip and somebody has to deal with the office work they leave behind. Or their boss insists on sending them on an external training course which similarly means there needs to be someone to look after affairs in their absence.

It makes far more sense to accept delegation as a necessary and worthwhile part of management than to wait until it is the only way out of an emergency. The senior executive who determines from the outset to build up a team of motivated and skilful employees who can take over in his absence and contribute bright ideas and new perspectives is going to lead a much less disruptive life than the macho manager who holds all the cards to his chest and believes that delegating anything but the most menial tasks is a sign of weakness and tantamount to relinquishing control.

This book is an attempt to describe ways in which delegation can be used to good effect to the benefit of the organisation and all who work in it. General tips on delegating in an enlightened way are outlined against the background of the new societal influences that are making delegation more essential than ever before.

2. Why Delegate?

Delegation is an attitude of mind. Theoretically it is not hard to do. After all, what could be simpler than handing over part of your workload to somebody else? But a lot of managers are reluctant to delegate for several reasons. One is the fear that the subordinate entrusted with the delegated work will make a mess of things. Such short-sighted managers often hide behind the much-quoted argument: 'If you want a job done properly, do it yourself.' The second is the obverse fear that the subordinate will make a better job of it! Both are a threat to the manager's progress in the organisation.

A third reason for managers' reluctance is that delegating properly can initially add to their workload and put even greater pressures on their limited time. One of the most frequent excuses put forward is: 'By the time I've explained it to Smith, I could have done it myself.'

It is certainly true that delegating all but the most menial tasks can be time-consuming at the outset. The manager will be familiar with all the background to the project to be handed over. The subordinate, if he or she stands any chance of performing the delegated project well, needs to be put in the picture. The manager will also have to explain what is the expected outcome of the delegated task and usually in what time-frame it should be completed.

The subordinate faced with an unfamiliar new duty might not immediately grasp all the complexities of what it entails and may find it necessary to go back to the manager several times to confirm that he or she is on the right track. This can be disruptive to the delegating manager and he might find it irritating to have to keep switching his concentration between the work he is currently undertaking and the guidance he is being called upon to give to the subordinate.

But if the manager is any good at delegating, these will be short-term problems and they will soon dissolve under the satisfaction of seeing a subordinate grow in his or her job, as well as the increasing pleasure of finding more time to focus on the leadership issues that are the prime responsibility of senior management.

As Bob Dixon, who runs courses on delegation at the Industrial Society, puts it: 'If you want to save time you have to invest time.'

Far from finding the ground taken away from under him, the senior manager who delegates effectively will find that the quality of his own work will steadily grow. He will also find that his company or division will start to run much more smoothly. The work of his subordinates will be greatly enhanced by virtue of the greater variety of tasks being passed down to them. Because they are undertaking broader tasks, the subordinates will derive more satisfaction from their work and will almost certainly do a better job simply because they are enjoying the challenge of new demands on their capabilities.

Because they are deriving more fulfilment from their work they can be expected to make a more worthwhile contribution. They are bound to invest more effort in enriching work than into the dull routine of the repetitive tasks they have been performing for a long time. These benefits are likely to raise standards throughout the entire company or division.

In addition, the subordinates will recognise the considerable degree of trust the delegating manager is showing in their capabilities and will feel they are a more significant part of the corporate team. This can only enhance the sense of *esprit de corps* and create the kind of relationships under which team work and the striving for excellence flourish.

Frederick Herzberg, the well-known American behavioural scientist, identified six key factors that motivate employees at work – what he called the six 'satisfiers'. These were achievement, responsibility, recognition, job growth, job interest and promotion. If delegation is effectively carried out it can satisfy all these six conditions.

The Route to Promotion

Another important advantage of delegating well is that it can help the delegator on the road to promotion. The ability to delegate is an essential part of leadership. Managers who demonstrate that they are good at delegating and that their organisations operate efficiently under a style of dispersed responsibility, can expect to be placed high on the shortlist of candidates for a more senior post.

The further up the organisation you go the more comprehensive your responsibilities are likely to be and the more need there will be to delegate effectively. It will become increasingly difficult to keep personal control of all aspects of your day-to-day managerial duties. The more you remove yourself from the technical detail, the more time you will have to concentrate on strategic issues that are vital to the future wellbeing of your organisation. Anyone whose record demonstrates delegation skills is well on the way to getting promoted.

Evidence of the truth of this statement is to be found in the career of Lord Tombs, the former chairman of Rolls-Royce:

I've always worked very hard at delegation on the principle that if you can get somebody else to do all the work, you are likely to be promoted. I always find that if you make spare time, if you organise yourself out of a job, nature doesn't like that; it gets filled up. People are too protective about delegation. They think they're weakening their position. I think they're strengthening it, because if they delegate properly they're running a tight outfit and they have time to take on more responsibility.

Tombs has two basic pieces of advice about delegation that he passes on to younger managers:

The first is the guy to whom you delegate will make mistakes you wouldn't have made yourself and that's why you are where you are and he's where he is. It's the nature of things. If you're senior, you would have done the job you've just left with more experience than the new man. The second, much more difficult, thing to accept is that the guy you delegate to will do things in a way you wouldn't have done and perhaps in better ways. That's tough to recognise. Whenever that has happened to me I've been delighted. I've learned from it.

The Switch to General Management

Delegation is particularly difficult for managers who have climbed an organisation through a single functional skill and are suddenly plunged into a general management job where they have to deal with a variety of different disciplines. The leading management schools all have training programmes that help executives cope with this difficult transition period, but adopting a new management style that is appropriate to this major career change is not easy in practice.

Delegation is one of the keys to making the transition successfully. Clearly, the new general manager has a lot to learn about the other disciplines that now become an integral part of his job and until he has mastered them he will be very dependent on the skills of the management team he is leading. He can demonstrate his willingness to delegate by authorising those more experienced than he is to deal with important decisions in the unfamiliar areas of his new responsibilities.

But he will also need to give up 'hands-on' control of his own speciality, since his new job will revolve mainly around strategic issues rather than the day-to-day running of the operation.

This is harder than it seems. When I (the author) was made managing editor of a business publication after spending much of my career as a lone-wolf journalist, I suddenly found myself in charge of an editorial team of 20 people of various skills and nationalities. From the beginning, I tried to encourage everyone to contribute ideas to help formulate the editorial strategy of the magazine.

A steady stream of editorial staff came into my office offering ideas and suggestions. But I found myself rejecting many of them because they had been tried before and failed. My repeated rejection of ideas began to sour the atmosphere of teamwork and shared experience that I had tried to foster. It then occurred to me that my approach was all wrong. Simply because ideas had been unsuccessful in the past did not mean they would fail next time around.

In the first place, they might have failed in the past because they had been tackled in the wrong way or simply because the times were not appropriate. Times change and what proves unpopular one year can be high fashion five years later. Reflecting on the situation persuaded me to change tack and I began to approve ideas that had previously fallen on barren ground. To my relief, many of the suggestions proved to be viable the second time around and the editorial team steadily gained confidence in my willingness to experiment with new approaches to old ideas.

I had learned an important lesson. Delegating doesn't simply mean sanctioning ideas you are absolutely certain will work. It means having confidence in other people's judgement and giving them the authority to go about things differently to the way you might have chosen. Obviously, when it becomes apparent that an idea is not working out and that too much time and energy is being put into something that stands little chance of reaping benefits, it is a leader's job to call it a day, even if that means temporarily disappointing and perhaps demoralising a subordinate.

Getting Things Done

The manager who makes the effort to delegate will eventually reap the rewards. What could be more satisfying than a smooth running organisation where the team works in harmony, each making a valuable contribution and each feeling a sense of job satisfaction? That in itself would be reward enough for the effort.

But it is in the self-interest of the manager to take delegation seriously. Apart from smoothing his path to promotion, it will also make his life much more bearable. We have all experienced the over-burdened executive with the bulging briefcase who burns the midnight oil at the office and takes home piles of work at the week-end because he is hogging everything to himself and is not prepared to risk letting others share his workload.

A log-jam of decisions piles up preventing others from doing their job properly simply because the reluctant delegator is unable to cope. It initially takes time to delegate effectively, but once it has become established practice, subordinates catch on fast. The log-jam clears and the organisation starts to operate like a well–oiled machine. Urgent decisions are not held up because the reluctant delegator is ensconced in a three-hour strategy meeting. Mountains of work awaiting action no longer stack up on his desk while he is on an overseas business trip. The work goes on in his absence in an atmosphere of trust and collaborative effort.

Assessment of Potential

By devolving responsibility, the senior manager will create the opportunity to assess the potential of his subordinates on a regular basis. Annual performance appraisals are all very well, but there is nothing to compare with setting your subordinates increasingly demanding tasks during the course of the year to learn to what extent they can be stretched and whether they have hidden talents that are not being brought out by the scope of their routine work.

There is inevitably an element of risk involved in asking subordinates to undertake demanding projects that are going to test their capabilities to the limit. But the old saying, nothing ventured nothing gained, was never more true than where delegation is concerned. Both you as the delegator and the subordinate who finds that he or she can cope with tasks they previously thought were beyond them will derive immense pleasure from the experience.

Indeed, probably one of the most important qualities of a leader is the ability to inspire others to scale heights they believed were beyond them. If they don't quite reach the summit, at least they will have come further in the attempt than if they had adhered rigidly to the confines of their routine job. By careful guidance and monitoring the delegating manager can limit the risks involved. With each new attempt to scale the mountain, both the delegating manager and the subordinate will become that much wiser. If they pace themselves carefully, failures will be minimal, successes will prevail.

SYMPTOMS OF THE NEED TO DELEGATE MORE

There are a number of clear symptoms that you are not delegating as effectively as you ought to be:

- *Do you regularly take work home with you in the evenings and at the week-ends?* A lot of managers believe that a bulging briefcase is a sign that they have an important job. But they know in their heart of hearts that the reason they have more work than they can cope with in office hours is because they are not on top of the job. They rationalise the situation by convincing themselves that they are undergoing a particularly intense period of their career and that given time they will get the job more under control. In the meantime, they will have to sacrifice their family and social life in order to ensure further career advancement. The truth is the situation will only get worse if the manager doesn't find some way to share his workload.

- *Do you work longer hours than those in your management team?* Many managers believe it is their duty to stay on at the office long after they have said good night to their subordinates. There is something macho about their powers of endurance and it demonstrates how dedicated they are to their work. When the boss passes their office and sees the lights are still burning well into the night, they believe their devotion to duty will be recognised by further promotion or an enhanced salary packet. In fact, they are almost certainly doing themselves more harm than good. Nobody can keep up such a gruelling work routine for long without ending up exhausted and stale. It is quite likely that the boss will consider the long hours worked as a sign that the manager is not on top of his job. He may even have second thoughts about keeping him in the present job, let alone considering promotion.

- *Do you have little time for appointments, recreation, study and social activities?* The more senior you become, the more people will seek your advice both inside and outside your organisation. Your experience and knowledge will be sought after by a variety of people and organisations. If you have no time to pass on your wisdom and experience to others, you will be failing to fulfil your full role in society. Charitable organisations and other good causes rely on experienced people to offer them advice and assistance. Similarly, within your own organisation an important part of your function is to pass on your experience to those who are still way down the learning curve.

- *Are you frequently interrupted at work because others come to you to discuss minor issues?* As a senior executive you should always try to be available when subordinates need advice on important issues and decisions. But an open door policy should not mean that everyone in the organisation feels free to step into your office whenever he or she wants to pass the time of day. A balance needs to be struck between friendliness and over familiarity. Frequent visits from subordinates almost certainly mean they are under-utilised and that insufficient tasks are being delegated to them.

- *Do your employees feel they have to consult you before they make every minor decision?* It makes many managers feel important when they are constantly consulted on decisions that could well be taken by their subordinates acting on their own initiative. It keeps the senior executive in the picture of what is happening in the organisation below, and the gratitude his subordinates display for his advice and reassurances gives him a warm feeling inside. But inevitably, while the senior executive is dealing with minor issues he cannot be concentrating on his own job properly. His work, which is vital for the well-being of the whole organisation, is bound to suffer.

- *Is a lot of unfinished work accumulating on your desk? Do you find it difficult to meet reasonable deadlines?* Managers often believe that having more work than they can cope with is only to be expected at their level of responsibility. The more important you are the busier you are likely to be. There are bound to be times when you become overwhelmed. But if you are consistently behind with your work and you are failing to meet deadlines which other people depend on, there is clearly something wrong with the way you are organising your job.

- *Do you seem to be constantly operating in a climate of crisis?* Many executives thrive on crises and get a kick out of solving problems in the eleventh hour. Working in such conditions certainly keeps the adrenalin flowing and it can be as exciting as being on the front line of a battlefield; but it has obvious dangers. There will come a time when the eleventh hour becomes the final hour and you will find you have run out of time. It is good neither for the blood pressure nor for the health of the organisation to be operating on tenterhooks the whole time. It is a sure sign that you are not spreading the load among your management team.

- *Do you spend more time working on details than on planning and supervising?* Most managers who have come up via a single functional discipline have spent the bulk of their time dealing with detail and building up their expertise. They find it difficult to switch to a different management style when they reach a general management post. It is a lot easier to carry on doing the things they were good at rather than attempting to tackle the more intangible duties of planning and supervising.

- *Do you lack confidence in your subordinates' abilities?* It is not uncommon for managers to justify holding on to work that ought to be delegated because they are convinced that they are the only people who can do it efficiently. After all, they rationalise to themselves, it was their technical expertise that led to them being promoted to their senior management job in the first place. That may be so, but their suitability for the next level of promotion is likely to be judged on entirely different criteria. At the same time, lack of faith in subordinates is very bad for morale. It also becomes a self-fulfilling prophecy. As soon as subordinates sense a lack of confidence in their capabilities they will only perform to the minimum requirements of their job. This will inevitably lead to work piling up on the senior executive's desk.

- *Do you hesitate to admit that you need help to keep on top of your job?* Turning to others for help is often seen as a sign of weakness. Many top managers like to give the impression that they are masters of all they survey. They are the person in charge so there is nothing they can't handle. This, of course, is a fallacy. One of the most important functions of a senior executive is to utilise and develop the skills of his management team. There will almost certainly be someone in your team who is more expert than you are on certain issues. Calling on their assistance will not only endorse your recognition of their special abilities; it will also reduce your load and enhance team spirit.

- *Do you neglect to seek ideas and suggestions from your staff?* Often, senior executives wrestle with difficult problems forgetting that they are backed up by a team of people who all have imaginations and good ideas. Calling a meeting of your team members every time you are faced with a knotty problem can be time-consuming and sometimes counter-productive. But it is surprising how many bright ideas evolve from a quick brainstorming session. Apart from *ad hoc* sessions to tackle unexpected problems, every senior executive ought to hold regular quarterly planning sessions with his or her key people to sound out all the ideas that are bouncing around the organisation which might easily pass the top man by when he is buried in his own work. Those who come up with the bright ideas ought to be rewarded by being delegated to tackle the projects you were finding it difficult to come to grips with.

WHY MANAGERS DON'T DELEGATE

Despite all the logical arguments in favour of delegation, many managers merely pay it lip service. Their conscious efforts to delegate are half-hearted at best. The reason is not difficult to understand. 'Managers very much want control. Wanting control and delegating are not really compatible,' says Jim Durcan, director of the leadership development programme at Ashridge Management College.

His views are echoed by Tony Knight, director of the strategic management programme at Henley Management College:

'Delegation generally is not well handled because people aren't skilled in knowing how to let go or how much control to retain, how to motivate people to do things on their own account while not apparently directing them in too much detail.'

Dr Barry Brown, a consultant psychologist at the Independent Assessment & Research Centre, defines delegation as 'arranging for allocation of control between people. It is to do with the distribution of power.' IARC assesses managers in relation to the purpose of the organisation they work for and its corporate structure. As part of that process, it measures managers' ability to delegate. One of the Centre's tests looks at how much personal control individual managers need to carry out their work, how much control they can tolerate from other people and to what extent they succeed in balancing the two.

Brown's research shows that finding the right control balance can be particularly difficult in organisations that have been de-layered.

Where the structure is flattening because the purpose of the business is shifting towards a much more responsive, custom-oriented service, the demands on the individual to balance control and power more evenly are much greater and for some people letting go of control is really problematic.

Trusting other people to do things as well as you would is a real problem for some people. There are some organisations in which allocation of power to the top encourages people to take complete control and to see that as valuable – as the right way to behave. It's not just macho. It's because 'I'm a good manager; I take responsibility for everything. I shoulder it'. It's a version of your being committed and your heart being in the right place; you take this company seriously; you really identify with the company and you don't abdicate responsibility. That's one of the counter-arguments often put up against delegation. In fact, it's totally misunderstanding the nature of delegation. What delegation ought to be is a sharing of power.

Ashridge Management College asks subordinates of managers on its courses to fill in a questionnaire about their perception of their boss's leadership style. Part of the survey covers delegation. In most cases the subordinates maintain that they don't recognise delegation as part of their boss's leadership style. When the bosses are confronted with these conclusions they usually react with hostility to the observation. They often defend themselves by saying that the questionnaire did not define delegation clearly enough.

When asked to describe under what circumstances they would delegate, they usually start talking vaguely about the need for a competent team of people in whom there would be total trust. Asked if they have people like that working for them, they usually evade the issue by saying something to the effect that they have only been in their present job for a short while.

Holding On

The problem starts at the top of the organisation. Senior managers are often reluctant to delegate because it has not been part of their own experience. Durcan maintains that even at board level senior executives are reluctant to delegate although it is a commonly held view that their prime function is to give strategic direction to the organisation. They simply cannot resist continuing to get involved in the kind of day-to-day issues that occupied them on their climb to the top of the hierarchy.

Tony Knight of Henley Management College, a telecommunications engineer by training, maintains the technologists are among the worst at delegating practical tasks:

> *You always want to be involved in the day-to-day activities. It is very difficult for such people to turn off and allow themselves to delegate that work to others. As an ex-engineer it's nice to get your hands on real things occasionally, but there comes a time when you have to do the managing and leave others to get on with it. That's quite a wrench.*

Dixon of the Industrial Society recalls some years ago visiting a small engineering company in Harrow employing about 30 people. When he arrived he was ushered into the office of the managing director, an astute engineer who had built the business up from nothing. To Dixon's astonishment, he found the managing director sitting at a drawing board in a corner of his office intently designing a product innovation. He kept Dixon waiting for quarter of an hour while he finished off what he was doing.

The managing director was unable to pull away from the skills that had enabled his company to flourish in the past. The company subsequently went into liquidation, because he held on to the technical work and had no time left to manage the organisation properly.

'Probably what he should have done,' suggests Dixon, 'was get in a professional business manager, which would have given him the time to spend on the creative side. Or he should have let go of the creative work, realising he had a business to manage. He couldn't have done both.'

Sheila Rothwell, head of the human resource faculty at Henley Management College, suggests that senior managers are reluctant to delegate because of fear of the unknown. They are often uncomfortable concentrating on strategy and future imponderables. 'The tendency is always to revert to managing what you know and doing the work of the people below you.'

The Funnel of Specialisation

This tendency to revert to what we are best at is sometimes referred to as the *funnel of specialisation*. By the time we leave school we have acquired a wide knowledge of a lot of subjects, but we don't know about any of them in great depth. We know a little about a lot. We then tend to specialise in our chosen subject by obtaining a degree or undergoing an apprenticeship in the profession of our choosing, for example. We become experts and because of our expertise we get promoted. We are recognised for our technical skill in a specialised area.

We climb the corporate hierarchy via the funnel of specialisation. But when we eventually become promoted to a general management position our experience starts to broaden again. We need to know a certain amount about a variety of disciplines. We need to get involved in such issues as people management, budgetary control and forward planning. But when life gets tough we tend to revert back to the narrow part of the funnel of specialisation, where we feel comfortable, instead of delegating the work to others. Bad delegators often justify this tendency by boasting that they are 'hands-on' managers and need to know what is going on below them.

Durcan notes that 'hands-on' has come to be regarded as a pejorative term. 'But if you say "immediate interest", "involvement with the business", "concern about customers", any of those sorts of things, then that puts it in a different perspective. You have to distinguish between what is currently popular in the management literature and that which managers actually do in practice.'

In Durcan's experience, there's a world of difference between what managers tell you they do and what their subordinates will tell you they do:

> *In theory top executives ought to be concerned with strategic decisions, they ought to have their hands off, they ought to be willing to delegate. That would have been true twenty years ago, let alone in the current climate. There are more pressing reasons in the current climate why you ought to take your hands off. But I think managers are often very scared to take their hands off for a whole series of reasons.*
>
> *Why did they get promoted? They got promoted because they were good at doing the job they were currently in. I know they shouldn't have been. I know they ought to have been promoted because they are going to be good at the job they're supposed to do next, but the reality is that most people get promoted because they are good at the job they already do. That leaves them with a real emotional commitment to that. They often find it very difficult to cut the umbilical cord – to actually let go.*

Under-employed

Another reason many senior executives persist in playing a hands-on role is that they are often under-employed simply because the strategic issues they ought to be involved with are not passed down to them from board level. Although divisional heads ought to be developing their own strategies since they are the ones who have to do the managing, too often corporate headquarters still pulls the strings. Notes Durcan:

> *There are very few who operate like Hanson, where the head office says: 'You've got two financial targets – get on with it. We are not interested in how you do it, we just want results'. When that doesn't happen,*

divisional executives spend most of their time playing games with those above them and interfering further down – partly because they like what they do further down and they are comfortable with it, and partly because most managers are obsessed about what they see as up-to-date information.

If he runs into a colleague in the corridor who says 'I think we've got a big problem with a major customer,' the senior executive immediately becomes Superman, springing into action, saying 'what can I do to assist? I used to know them; I worked with those. Let me at them; I'll talk to them', instead of saying 'So what are you going to do about it?'

Stuck with Accountability

All the theorists espouse the view that delegation is important because it enables managers to free up their time to get on with the issues that are of paramount importance in their job. At the same time, delegation will develop and grow the people working under them. Both these views are indisputable, provided managers are careful to delegate work that stretches the subordinate and not just the irritating tasks they don't want to be bothered with themselves.

Managers are stuck with the dilemma that they can delegate authority but they can't delegate accountability. You can pass down a task to someone to do on your behalf, but in the end, if the subordinate fouls up, it is the manager who is made accountable. The buck stops with him.

On the course run by the Industrial Society, three principal aspects of delegation are examined – responsibility, authority and accountability. There is often considerable confusion about the difference between authority and accountability. Explains Bob Dixon: 'Our argument is that responsibility is given to the person being delegated to, as is authority in that the person is going to be making the decisions that you normally make. Therefore, you have to pass on the authority. But at the end of the day the delegator is still accountable.'

Dixon stresses that delegation is much more than simply allocating a group of tasks to subordinates:

It is not unusual for people to talk about delegation when they actually mean allocation. It is not allocation; neither is it abdication. Delegation does involve risk. When you think about it, you are actually giving away the thing you would like to retain (the authority) and you retain the thing you would like to give away (the accountability).

Failures of the Reward System

Another constraining factor is the question of whether managers feel they are rewarded for developing their subordinates. If you asked most executives how much time they put into developing their immediate staff, the chances are they would say that is the responsibility of the human resources division. Observes Durcan:

I think that reflects a concern by many senior executives about whether the organisation they work for really values those who grow and develop talent. I know they will tell you that in human resource policy documents. But ultimately how is success measured in a particular organisation? Is success measured by the number of good people who worked for you over the years or is it measured by the ability to put dollars on the bottom line? I think very often organisations, despite the formal statements, do not in fact promote people because they are seen to have identified and developed talent. They promote people because they are said to have good hands-on experience.

There's a powerful case for managers really caring about delegation, really trying to select the right people and not just in the sense of finding all-stars, but seeing who's available to them, seeing what talents they've got, seeing how you can develop those talents, melding them into a team to perform effectively. All that's fine. My question is: Does the organisation reward system recognise this? If it doesn't, I would argue that it is likely to be a fairly low priority. Very often organisational reward systems do not actually significantly reward people who treat delegation seriously.'

Personality Traits

In Rothwell's view the ability to delegate has a lot to do with personality. Some people are better at coaching than others. Some people prefer to delve into detail when they ought to be leaving their subordinates to get on with the job. Suggests Rothwell:

To some extent promotional processes ought to sort this out. People who get promoted to the highest levels should be the people with the ability to let go and the ability to see the wood from the trees and manage their own time and their own priorities, but it doesn't always work out like that.

Daring to sit and think

One of the constraints on the willingness to delegate The Industrial Society has identified is what it calls 'daring to sit and think'. In theory, delegating technical work to subordinates leaves the senior manager time to reflect on the future course of the organisation. But sitting and thinking is a visibly inactive preoccupation. Most managers are driven by the Protestant work ethic. The most evident sign that someone is working is a lot of activity.

The manager who is sitting back in his office chair with his hands behind his head gazing into space may be dreaming up ideas that are going to make all the difference to the future success of the organisation. But to observers he is merely idling his time away. If his boss takes that view of it he is likely to be in trouble. For that reason, we often put on an act of being busy simply to convince everyone that we are doing something productive. Observes Dixon:

'It's not only that others will feel you are not pulling your weight; you feel you're not pulling your weight yourself, because there is no visible sign that you are actually working. You have to come to terms with that as an individual.'

Being on top of things

Many managers shy away from delegation because they feel it will prevent them from being on top of what is happening in their particular organisation. They are concerned that if they delegate important projects to subordinates there will be long periods when they are not fully conversant with how things are progressing. They are especially worried that when their boss asks them how things are developing they will not appear to be in control if they have to investigate the position before they can provide an answer.

The problem is that in order to keep abreast of what is happening with a particular project it will mean constant meetings with the subordinate to obtain updates. This is not only very time consuming and to a large extent obviates the reason for delegating the task; it will also give the subordinate the impression that the senior manager is less than convinced the task will be performed to the expected standard. It will seem to the subordinate that the manager is breathing down his neck all the time or indulging in what is sometimes known as *parrot delegation* – sitting on the subordinate's shoulder and monitoring everything that is done while it happens.

Squandering Secretaries' Talents

One of the most squandered areas of delegation is the efficient use of secretaries. Henley Management College has made a study of how effectively secretarial and clerical skills are employed in UK companies. It concluded that secretaries are very under-utilised in comparison with their true potential. Notes Rothwell:

> *They are very much tied to an individual manager in many cases and how a manager sees that person developing. The secretaries may get promoted with the manager, but they don't necessarily get promoted as part of a structured career planning programme. In de-layered organisations secretaries have often got more of the skills the organisation needs – networking skills, the ability to handle technology, knowing a wide range of people.*

Catapulted into Delegation

Often the first time executives really give serious thought to delegation is when they are obliged to attend a lengthy management course. Rothwell notes that courses are often the trigger for introducing more structured delegation procedures. The course participants realise they are going to be away for four to six weeks and that everything will grind to a halt unless they delegate a lot of the work they are accustomed to hogging to themselves. Once they have woken up to the necessity, they are greatly relieved and often admit it is something they should have done years ago.

For some, the effort of passing their work on to others while they are away on a management course can be quite traumatic.

Rothwell cites the example of one manager who was 'worried sick' at the prospect of having to hand over his responsibilities while at Henley. He cancelled his attendance at the college three times before finally summoning up the courage to delegate his work to someone else.

The manager was operating in the field of heavy engineering contracts and he had no faith that his second in command could handle the work in his absence. His deputy was apparently very skilled on the technical side, but had little experience of dealing with contracts, which were the lifeblood of the company. To allay his fears, the reluctant delegator brought in a more junior manager to stand in for him during his absence at Henley, he was so convinced his second-in-command would not be able to cope.

This raised the question of why the contracts manager had never brought the shortcomings in this critical part of the job to the attention of his No. 2. Was it because the senior manager enjoyed being the sole expert in this area? It perhaps gave him a sense of power. Or was it that it had never occurred to him that his deputy would some day have to step into his shoes? Apparently, sitting down with his second in command and discussing how his weakness could best be overcome had never occurred to the senior manager.

Powers of Persuasion

All the textbooks on delegation stress the importance of giving a subordinate the authority as well as the responsibility for a delegated task. This is not always as straightforward as it seems. Bernard Taylor, professor of business policy at Henley Management College, believes that 'a lot of muddled thinking goes on' about delegation. 'There's an attempt to hold people responsible for things they cannot run.'

Taylor points out that often managers do not have control over all the decisions and actions they need to take. They may not control the budget, for example; they may not be in a position to decide the salary scales of their subordinates; they may have little control over working conditions.

The Henley professor cites an example that came to light when he was advising the former National Coal Board. There was an attempt to make colliery managers semi-autonomous managing directors of the mines they ran. But when the level of control they had over their operations was examined, it transpired that they were little more than production managers. They had no control over prices, wages or the purchase of mining equipment, for example. These were all handled centrally.

This, in Taylor's view, means that managers need to develop strong powers of persuasion if they are to succeed in carrying out many of the duties delegated to them: 'I believe the responsibility of managers is not only to take decisions but to influence the decisions of other people and therefore there is a large political element in management. You influence upwards, sideways and downwards and even if you cannot legally take a particular decision, you have to do your level best to influence that decision.'

Only Bad Subordinates

Turning the whole issue on its head, Barry Curnow, a former president of the Institute of Personnel Management, holds the somewhat controversial view that there is no such thing as a bad delegator. There are only bad subordinates. He argues that the onus is on the subordinate to ensure that the appropriate amount of delegation takes place. Curnow, who runs his own London-based training centre, maintains that subordinates, particularly in the higher reaches of an organisation, ought to take more initiative in the way they support their bosses:

> I would be the first to acknowledge that if you have a boss who is one hundred per cent determined not to delegate it's a no-go area. But most bosses aren't that way inclined. It's pretty pathetic if someone who is paid £40,000 to £50,000 a year is complaining because their boss, who earns £70,000, is not delegating enough. It's the psychology of the kindergarten.

Curnow suggests subordinates ought to demonstrate more forcibly to their bosses that they have 'the ability, competence and readiness to do a wider range to things, because that's what those subordinates are paid for. I don't want to push the Japanese analogy because it's a very different situation, but the one thing they show is a commitment to the wider organisational purpose, however it may be seen or defined.'

In Curnow's view, subordinates need to show more sensitivity and understanding of their bosses' situation by not bombarding them with requests for greater responsibility but by 'exercising critical judgement and understanding what it's like to be in the boss's job, which includes judgement about restraint, timing, pace and appropriateness.'

Overcoming Resistance to Delegation

However strong their reluctance to delegate, senior managers should force themselves to overcome the resistance in four main areas:

- *Lack of confidence in subordinates' competence.* If you have no faith in your subordinates' abilities, start by delegating relatively minor tasks where subordinates' mistakes will have negligible impact. Gradually introduce more demanding assignments as your confidence grows.
- *Desire for perfection.* If you are convinced that you are the only person capable of performing a task to the desired level of competence, start by delegating tasks that do not demand this degree of perfection. At the same time, you can coach subordinates to help increase their skills, leaving you free to tackle those assignments which only you are equipped to perform.
- *Insufficient time to explain the details of the assignment.* This may be an acceptable reason for failing to delegate short-term projects or one-off assignments. However, in the case of longer-term or repetitive tasks, taking the trouble to teach employees tasks will save time in the long run.
- *Holding on to the more satisfying tasks.* If you find a particular task fulfilling or you receive recognition from others when you perform it well, there is a tendency to reserve it for yourself

when you ought to be thinking about delegating it. To overcome this tendency, look for higher level tasks which give you as much satisfaction and recognition. By developing your own accomplishments you may derive even greater satisfaction.

Fallacies of delegation

1. Delegating takes too much time.
2. Nobody can do this job as well as I can.
3. If I hand over my responsibilities to somebody else I will be working myself out of a job.
4. If I risk entrusting a subordinate with this important work we could end up losing a vital customer.
5. I wouldn't have been given this job if somebody else was capable of doing it for me.
6. OK, I'll pass some of my work down the line, but nothing that is going to put me or this company at risk.
7. I won't know what's been happening when I talk to the customer.
8. I like to keep my hand in with this sort of work (i.e. I enjoy it and don't want to give it up to anyone else!)

Benefits of delegating

1. Leaves delegator free to concentrate on more important strategic issues
2. Increases job satisfaction for delegator and subordinate
3. Helps subordinate to develop new skills
4. Helps subordinate to grow in confidence
5. Provides an opportunity to assess subordinates' potential
6. Fosters teamwork
7. Helps create a more motivated workforce
8. Enhances morale
9. Improves communication through feedback
10. Creates fresh insights into work issues
11. Helps create a climate for achievement

12. Ultimately speeds up results
13. Reduces costs (subordinate's time is less expensive than delegator's time)
14. Increases chances of promotion for delegator
15. Ensures smooth succession when delegator is promoted

3. The Climate for Delegation – New Influences

According to Tom Peters, the celebrated American business guru, we are in the midst of the most dramatic transformation in the way human beings organise themselves since the Chinese invented the pyramidal command structure 2,000 years ago. The flattening of the pyramid, globalisation, networking, teleworking, a better educated workforce, less job security and a leadership vacuum are all contributing to a new look at the way delegation is performed.

Less autocratic organisations mean that the conventional way of passing instructions down the line is no longer appropriate. A more demanding workforce with higher motivational expectations is calling for a review of the boss–subordinate relationship and the degree of authority that can be devolved to junior employees.

Bernard Taylor, professor of business policy at Henley Management College, believes this country is undergoing a revolution in management both in the public and private sector. 'A characteristic of this revolution is that there is an attempt to hold people accountable and responsible for clearly defined areas of management,' he adds.

The trend towards devolved responsibility can be found in a whole variety of examples in the private and public sector. Hospitals and groups of doctors are opting out of direct control of the National Health Service and are running their own affairs. Schools and polytechnics are also going it alone, echoing the enterprise culture that has epitomised the private sector in the past decade. They are controlling their own budgets and managing their own activities. Observes Taylor:

There's an attempt to establish profit centres and to segregate businesses into discrete units where a team of managers is responsible for a hospital, a school or a public health area. This is part of the Thatcher revolution in Britain and it is only just beginning to be felt in the public service sector where management historically hasn't been the priority. The priority has always been policy-making and advising the Minister answering parliamentary questions.

By launching his Citizen's Charter, Prime Minister John Major has lent new impetus to the trend towards devolved responsibility. The Civil Service has set in motion a new, more commercial approach that is expected to change radically the relationship between government and its employees. The new management style sweeping through Whitehall was summed up by Sir Robin Butler, head of the Civil Service, in a television interview:

The government and Civil Service is a huge and complex organisation, from social security benefits to vehicle testing to printing passports. That can't all be organised by a minister these days. It can't be organised by me, so the philosophy behind it is to drive down, to delegate powers to take decisions, as close as possible to the point of delivery.

Typical of the changes taking place is the new approach in the benefits service. Benefits offices used often to be battle grounds between staff and claimants. Now a new attitude is pervading them. Claimants are being treated as customers and their needs are coming first. Benefits staff are being required to work to customer service targets, which means payments must be made quickly and with more accuracy. In order to meet these targets staff must be free to take initiatives. Michael Richard, chief executive of the Benefits Agency, explains:

People at every level from supervisor to senior management want more responsibility, more freedom to take decisions and not actually be governed, if you like, by what was a very bureaucratic top-heavy management and I think although some people found these changes uncomfortable, particularly those who got very used to being told how to do something, to refer to instructions and so on, I think the vast majority more than appreciate the changes that have happened.

The Benefits Agency has introduced a massive computerisation programme to cut down on the mountains of paperwork. This is expected also to contribute to the breaking down of its traditional hierarchical culture. The computers are giving junior staff access to the kind of information they need to make decisions, whereas before they had to consult management about every move.

A similar revolution is taking place at the Central Middlesex Trust Hospital, which is undergoing one of the most radical experiments ever seen in a British hospital. For the first time, individual consultants and ward sisters are being handed control over budgets and being told to trade with each other within the hospital. By devolving financial responsibility to medical staff the hospital hopes to cut the cost of treatment. Sister Jennie Hillier now runs the budget for the hospital's two orthopaedic wards. To pay for staff and other costs she has to sell beds in the ward to consultants who book space for their patients.

Such radical shifts in the way public sector organisations are run will inevitably throw up problems about responsibility and accountability, but those at the top of the Civil Service are convinced that the idea of giving greater authority to the staff at the local level will lead to major improvements in efficiency and productivity. Says Sir Robin Butler:

It's the same in any large company. You do want to give people who are serving the customer the responsibility to do that well, not feeling they have always got to be told how to do it by somebody from above them. But you've also got to retain the line of accountability right up to the top to the chairman, through the chairman to the shareholders. You have to do that in a private company and similarly in government you must retain that line of accountability up to ministers and through ministers to Parliament.

The impact of this management revolution on traditional approaches to delegation is immense. Delegation, according to Taylor, 'now penetrates right into the heart of management.'

Although the basic skills of delegation remain the same (as described in Chapter 5), the climate for devolved responsibility is undergoing rapid changes. The good news is that most of the influences are for the good. The need to delegate is becoming increasingly vital and there is a discernible trend towards delegating to develop the individual as well as improve the efficiency of the organisation.

LESS AUTOCRATIC ORGANISATIONS – THE FLATTENING OF THE PYRAMID

For years management gurus have been predicting the demise of autocratic management and the pyramidal organisation structure. The pyramid has taken a long time to crumble. The ancient Chinese invented it as a way to pass instructions down the line and information up to the top. It has been adopted by the military, the Church and latterly by public services and commercial organisations.

Several decades ago American leadership guru Warren Bennis was convinced that autocratic management would be replaced by what he called *adhocracy* – spontaneous project groups set up to tackle management problems as and when they arose. Today he is less certain that bureaucracy is at its last gasp:

'I can't say bureaucracies don't exist any more because they clearly do. But it does seem to me that there are more organisations based on task forces, networking and all forms of more organic, adaptive structures.'

In recent years, particularly in the US, there have been numerous experiments with new organisational shapes to replace the omnipresent pyramid. The new structures have rejoiced in wonderfully evocative names like *the beehive, the bell, the doughnut* and *the bicycle wheel*. They have all had much the same aim of moving away from the sharp-pointed pyramid with its traditional hierarchical approach to management.

There was even one experiment in the US that tried to discard a formal organisation structure entirely. One company temporarily put all its employees on a level footing. There were no senior or junior managers. Everyone enjoyed equal status. It was virtually management by anarchy. However, the general trend away from autocratic structures has been less revolutionary in the UK. The main outcome in this country has been for the pyramid to become flattened as many companies have striven to reduce their layers of management to take account of new technology and to cut costs. In the past few years major corporations like BP, BT and the Post Office have cut out huge swathes of middle management to produce leaner, more competitive organisations. It seems inevitable that the flattening process will continue as middle managers become more and more squeezed. Notes Tom Peters, co-author of the bestseller *In Search of Excellence*:

> *Whole new shapes of organisation are starting to emerge. Look at the new upstarts in Great Britain, to some extent, and in the US, to a great extent, and they just don't look like yesterday's companies in any way, shape or form. The way people look, smell and spend their day is not the way they have done so for perhaps the last couple of thousand years.*

A number of companies, like Rank Xerox and Digital Equipment Corp., have inverted the traditional pyramid organisation structure in an attempt to devolve responsibility and authority to those closest to the customer. The senior managers who were formerly at the apex of the pyramid have been turned into support staff, whose main function now is to coach and counsel the front-line staff and the members of self-managed work groups. The topsy-turvy environment that Digital Equipment now lives in can cause some confusion when trying to explain it to the outside world. Elaborates Alistair Wright, human resource director of its Reading-based UK subsidiary:

'What we are actually trying to do is delegate authority to the lowest level or the highest level possible, whichever way you look at it.'

The trend now is away from focusing on discrete divisions towards taking a systemic and holistic view of organisations. The division of labour philosophy of Frederick Taylor is being replaced by a view of organisations that concentrates on integration of the whole and the interaction of the various parts. Observes Wright of Digital Equipment:

> *The way organisations were designed – and still are designed today – was based on an analytical approach. The whole organisation was carved up into its component parts – personnel, finance, sales servicing, manufacturing and so on. People then focused on the bits to try to optimise them. What we are beginning to understand now is that's not the way to approach it at all. The way to approach it is to regard the integration between the bits as being the most powerful issue. We call it boundary management. By understanding where your system touches another system you can actually interface and interact with it better.*

Replacing Bureaucracy at BP

Within weeks of taking over as the new chairman of BP in 1990, Robert Horton was announcing sweeping organisational changes aimed at transforming the giant oil company. In place of the former culture of bureaucracy, constant second-guessing, and extreme distrust, Horton set out to create a structure with the minimum of controls and the maximum delegation of responsibility, plus a supporting culture of openness, informal communication and verve. Christopher Lorenz, writing in the *Financial Times*, pointed out that rather than simply establishing a shallower, flatter, more efficient version of the existing pyramid, Horton wanted to develop an organisation that worked, thought and felt entirely different.

Horton's resignation in June 1992 after the announcement of poor trading figures and rumours that there was growing acrimony between him and other members of the board, raises questions about whether he tried to bring about changes too swiftly and without sufficient awareness of the bitter resistance he might come up against among traditionalists in BP. However, BP's problems are unlikely to deter other companies from travelling a similar road in the search for more efficient and democratic methods of organisation.

The main impetus for flattening the pyramid has been the drive for greater efficiency and productivity. American management guru Peter Drucker has pointed out that while manufacturing productivity in the west has increased 45-fold (about four per cent a year) in the past 120 years, white collar productivity has hardly increased at all. The computer has not made a blind bit of difference. It has merely replaced lines of clerks carrying out manual tasks with lines of programmers.

At the same time, most companies have pared back their blue collar workforce as far as is practical. The next target – and the one that is being fiercely pursued at the moment – is cutting back on middle management. Observes Adrian Savage of Assessment Design Services, the Leamington Spa training agency:

> A lot of organisations have chopped and chopped at junior levels until there really isn't too much left. The next obvious place to go for is the middle levels. When you chop out the middle levels you get the flattening of the pyramid and in those circumstances people are forced to delegate.

Jim Durcan, who runs the leadership development programme at Ashridge Management College, agrees:

> I don't want to go overboard on the way organisations have changed, but I think it is probably realistic to say a significant number of organisations have attempted to take out layers of middle management in recent years with varying degrees of success. There are still pyramids, but they are much flatter.
>
> That sort of organisational shift clearly creates more scope for delegation and decentralisation. You could argue the more you flatten the pyramid the more you have a critical need for empowerment at lower levels. If they are all at the bottom level saying: 'it's not my job, you never told me to do that', you can find yourself in a real mess, because

you no longer have the managerial resources to tell everyone what to do. So I think the pressures there are really quite strong.

Although the flattening of the pyramid is forcing managers to delegate more, it does not necessarily mean they are delegating in the right way, in Savage's view:

The trouble is they're only forced to delegate tasks; they're not forced to delegate well; they are not forced to delegate to learn. They ought to be because only that way is the organisation going to be able to cope effectively. You've now got a lot of highly over-worked middle managers who maybe have responsibilities twice, three times, as great as they had in the past and are trying to tackle them in the same way. They go into the office at seven in the morning and stay at work until nine o'clock at night.

Savage cites the example of an over-worked manager at an accountancy practice. At the end of the day she would personally check all the letters that had been written by her staff. Her reason for doing so was that her staff made spelling mistakes and their grammar was not all that it should be. It took her two hours at the end of a busy day to check all the letters. Observers Savage:

She could not grasp that as long as she did it they weren't going to do it. Why should they bother? She was going to check it anyway. When she had a much smaller job her practice had been to check everything. Now her job had expanded she kept on doing the same thing, so more and more of her time was taken up checking the spelling and English of everyone who worked in her office.

Some companies have dispensed with the middle management function altogether. Sherwood Computer Services, a London-based software company, has turned its entire organisation into self-managed client teams that report directly to the top management board. (See case study in Chapter 10.)

Since it is generally recognised that the cost of an average manager to his company is three times his annual salary, the scope for financial savings in restructuring exercises of this kind are considerable.

One of the outcomes of the flatter pyramid is that it is much easier for top managers to find out what is going on further down in the organisation without having to wade through layers of command. On the other hand, with the advent of the lap-top computer and other technological innovations there is a lot more information available and senior executives tend to get swamped with it. Observes Savage:

> *Whereas before when a little bit of information finally worked its way up the hierarchy it was probably quite important, now huge computer print-outs land on top managers' desks and most of it is not really of any great importance.*

Because most top managers have climbed the hierarchy via a functional specialism, they are inclined to enjoy gathering a lot of data to further their expertise. Notes Savage:

> *All their experience has been being an expert – the one who has the knowledge and the information. That's hard to give up, so they tend to go on trying to amass knowledge and information. They wade through these huge computer printouts and such-like, bogging themselves down for ages. What they really should be doing is thinking about where the organisation is going. All the books tell you this. They don't do it.*
>
> *They can convince themselves they are terribly busy and they are doing terribly important things, but that's when they really should be delegating.*

One multinational where the people at the top were being totally swamped by vast amounts of information now manages its organisation on the basis of just three indicators. It worked out that these three areas were the ones that really mattered to the organisation and they were the only areas that the people at the top really needed to know about. It gave the company's top management a unique opportunity to clear the decks and delegate a whole mass of irrelevant work.

THE GROWTH OF TELEWORKING

The growth of teleworking is also challenging traditional organisation structures and methods of control. Teleworkers operate most or part of their time at a distance from the office, often from home, using modern telecommunications equipment. According to an estimate by The National Economic Development Office, around 1.5 million people are teleworking in the UK – one in 17 of the workforce.

The Henley Centre for Forecasting predicts that over 4 million people could become 'teleworkers' by the middle of this decade. Extrapolation from that prediction would indicate that by the year 2000 as many as one-third of the entire workforce could be back where they were 200 years ago in the early days of the industrial revolution – working from home as part of a cottage industry.

Professor John Stanworth and Celia Stanworth, writing in *Personnel Management* magazine, caution that such estimates are probably gross exaggerations, particularly as 'teleworking' is a much abused term and often confused with people who merely work from a home base. However, it is reasonable to assume that an increasing number of organisations is likely to employ teleworking as an alternative to the traditional office environment. This, as the authors of the *Personnel Management* article, point out, will require a significant change to a more open type of management control:

> There needs to be a shift from managing input (controlling methods of working) to managing output (i.e. judgement by results). The freeing of work from traditional locational and time constraints appears to pose a difficult problem for managers and supervisors to come to terms with. They often wish to continue to control hours of work rather than grant autonomy to homeworkers over their time and thus fully exploit the potential flexibility of telecommuting.
>
> Delegation skills are needed when managing 'distance' workers, and

this requires an ability to trust an individual to complete a task after jointly agreeing objectives and methods.

Liz Donaldson, writing in *The Independent*, points out that the growth in teleworking is causing thousands of managers to re-evaluate their role:

Office workers toiling at one remove from headquarters are no longer being judged by the traditional visual checks on attendance and time-serving, but by the results they produce.

Teleworking with its promise of huge productivity gains, also chimes with other managerial changes in the public sector, such as the wider use of performance measures, devolution of responsibility and setting of standards and targets to meet Citizen's Charter pledges.

The London Borough of Enfield introduced teleworking in May 1989 specifically to cope with the poll tax. Stuart Dennison, the assistant director of finance, counselled that teleworking is a two-way process. The right workers, high in self-discipline, need to be matched with capable managers who are strongly motivated to make the scheme succeed. Dennison told *The Independent*: 'Managers have to overcome a fear of losing control. A lot of people feel they are not in control unless they see an army of desks.'

Oxfordshire County Council also introduced its 'Flexiplace' scheme in 1989. Around 20 professionals in the trading standards department were given the opportunity to opt, with their manager's agreement, for quiet study or report-writing periods at home, during office hours. Roy Hill, assistant chief for trading standards, stressed that successful implementation required 'a great deal of trust' on both sides. Tasks must be devolved with more pre-planning. Managers have to learn to resist the temptation to make frequent checks on staff working away from the office and switch their attention firmly to results produced.

BT's Pioneering Experiment

British Telecom has launched a pioneering experiment in the Highlands of Scotland by providing the facilities for ten women handling directory inquiry calls to operate from their homes. The operators have had electronic terminals installed in their homes to provide a link with the BT centre in Inverness. A few buttons on a computer keyboard give them access to BT's entire directory of numbers.

. A key feature of the experiment is a video phone to help counter any sense of isolation the operators may feel.

BT's pioneering move is expected to pave the way for numerous similar experiments. Ticket agencies, insurance firms, mail order businesses, credit checking agencies and businesses handling large numbers of invoices are among the many organisations that lend themselves to teleworking.

Flexible Working at Digital Equipment

There is a strong tradition of flexible working at Digital Equipment, the leading computer manufacturer. In 1987, it started to explore the idea of introducing teleworking facilities for various groups within the company. It had already run several successful teleworking schemes for individuals. The idea now was to see if the same approach could be applied to complete departments. A pilot scheme was launched with its sales training department in Reading.

The training team comprises sales people who are seconded for a two year period to Reading from various UK regions. This particular group of Digital staff were selected because they highlighted a number of issues that had become apparent when investigating the advantages of teleworking. The training people were hardly ever in the office, but had been allotted office space that was costing the company around £7,000 per person per year. The sales trainers were rarely able to see their families during the two year secondment period, apart from exhausting week-end commuting. There was evidence that they could be 40 per cent more productive working more flexibly.

The manager of the group took the initiative to organise a series of workshops to explore the idea of working from home. Nine of the 13 members of the group decided to become home based. The manager of the group also decided to work from home and subsequently proved that it is possible to supervise remotely, provided the right support facilities are in place. Explains Phil Scott, Digital Equipment's human resource consultant:

It was decided the manager of the group was not going to carry out any more task management. She was going to be solely responsible for managing people. Because they were remotely based, it was very important for them to make sure they were always in touch, not just with the office, but with everybody else in the group. They had an administrator who was quite rigorous and insisted that they not just keep their diaries up to date, but she made sure they phoned her twice a day so she could pass on messages whenever they weren't coming into the office.

It was also decided there should be a compulsory meeting with the entire group at least once a fortnight, partly for work reasons and partly for socialising. The group set their own work standards to be measured by and it stipulated that it would not accept anyone new into the group in future who was not prepared to become a teleworker.

The success of this experiment has encouraged Digital Equipment to look much more closely at the infrastructure needed to support teleworking. It has also led the company to explore the whole idea of 'total location independent working.' Elaborates Scott:

If you tell people they have to be a teleworker that's almost as inflexible as telling them they have to work in an office all the time. We had also found that even when people were based in the office they were only using their desks about 14 per cent of the year. You can't really afford to have real estate lying dormant like that. So we needed to get to the point where we could offer people the ability to be location-independent.

We needed to give people the ability to be in the office part of the time, at home part of the time, work from a caravan in the Lake District, work in a train, wherever they wanted to be, and of course the computer technology was helping us to do that.

When a few years ago, one of Digital Equipment's main office blocks in Basingstoke burned to the ground and had to be re-built, the company seized the opportunity to incorporate a number of high-technology innovations that are helping to facilitate ever more ingenious forms of flexible working. The innovations include computer-integrated telephony which enables employees to lock their personal telephone number into a terminal so that it follows them wherever they go to in the building. The company is exploring the possibility of extending this facility to outside locations, thus overcoming the problem of those left in the office being plagued with calls for absent colleagues.

Slow Progress

Sheila Rothwell, of Henley Management College, believes that the relatively slow growth of teleworking stems as much from managers' fears and lack of flexibility as from any technical constraints. In an article she compiled for *Personnel Management* magazine she outlined the special delegation skills teleworking demands. On the one hand, managers must learn to 'let go' and trust the individual to complete the task and to request assistance where needed. On the other hand, they need to specify the task or the objectives to be met as clearly and accurately as possible.

In 'job' terms, suggests Rothwell,

> this may range from specification of objectives right down to details of the methods by which these are to be achieved. It is also likely to include specification of time scales and may include place, materials, people and other criteria for decision-making as well.
>
> The difficulty of doing this accurately is considerable, particularly in an area in which neither the manager nor anyone else may have much personal expertise or experience.

THE IMPACT OF NETWORKING

Networking, with its aptitude for developing a chain of co-operative relationships and informal alliances across international organisations, promises to undermine traditional reporting systems.

It is being facilitated by ever more sophisticated information technology that makes it possible to communicate globally at the touch of a button.

Managing relationships outside the formal chain of command calls for some special characteristics and interpersonal skills. These include personal initiative; willingness to share leadership; and willingness to take risks in expressing ideas and sharing information.

Part of the radical reorganisation spearheaded by Horton at BP involved the introduction of informal networks to replace the many departments, committees and management layers that previously characterised the group. These were intended to encompass people both at head office and out in the businesses. Christopher Lorenz wrote in the *Financial Times* at the time of the proposed changes:

> *The new arrangement will include not only permanent teams, but flexible ones pulled together from across BP's various businesses in order to carry out temporary tasks. The networking concept, which Horton calls 'the corporate glue', will be all-important to BP's continued ability to operate as an integrated corporation once it has completed the slashing back of committees and corporate staff.*

BOC, the international gases to medical equipment group, positively encourages networking. It expects its managers and technologists throughout the world to take on their shoulders the responsibility of accessing group technology wherever it resides, and to keep themselves apprised of, and to implement, best practices in every aspect of their businesses.

Encouraging informal networks has meant that BOC has had to review its head office function. Dick Giordano, BOC's former chairman, outlined this changed role in his 1990 Stockton Lecture to the London Business School:

> *Our job at the centre is to facilitate comunication and occasionally to audit. We keep a road map at the centre; a written and up-to-date technical inventory, telling us where the technology is and how it works rather than complete specifications for implementation.*

The centre issues publications, sponsors seminars and creates temporary committees to draw BOC managers' attention to what is available and what is changing. It appoints 'lead houses' for specific areas of technology or operational problems. A lead house maybe in Sydney or Osaka, but will be identified as the most knowledgeable within the group on that subject. 'It would have special responsibilities for dissemination of that knowledge to other group members around the world. We don't expect the work to be duplicated by other group companies.' Overall, the small number of staff at the centre in Britain act on occasion as a 'traffic policeman, sometimes as an orchestra conductor, and very often as a cheer leader.'

BOC does not underestimate the effort that is necessary to build up and sustain a networking organisation, one that it defines as valuing speed and flexibility and which, above all else, recognises that delay is costly and sometimes fatal. Giordano pointed out that such an organisation requires the managers to live with more than average ambiguity and sometimes conflicting objectives:

> *In a sense, we are asking managers to be schizophrenic. In dealing with competitors outside the walls of the group, we employ all the metaphors of war and sport: win and lose, cut and thrust, go for the jugular and others even more colourful. Within the company we expect them to change garments and co-operate in a benign fashion. Not all managers are this flexible.*

BOC has also come to recognise the important role that non-managerial staff play in a networking organisation. Often the links in the network are sustained by technical and functional personnel. This means that their quality and experience are increasingly important to the success of the business, giving BOC the challenge of fashioning rewards that reinforce their importance and allow them to develop careers outside the conventional corporate pyramid.

Not So New
Jim Durcan of Ashridge points out, however, that networking is not quite the new concept that a lot of people believe:

'Networking has always been around in organisations as a system of informal influence. It has always been possible to find people who have much more influence than their apparent position in the hierarchy would signal.'

Durcan quotes the example of a middle manager who was constantly asked for advice by colleagues at his own level, below his level and occasionally above his level. The reason was that the middle manager was well wired across the organisation. He had a real feel for what happened in the company and for which way the strategy was moving, what the hot issues were – simply because he was well connected and he had worked at it over the years.

The more people observed what was happening the more they felt they ought to check things out with this man before they embarked on a particular course of action. This really was power without any sort of responsibility. At one level the middle manager found it highly amusing. At another level it began to irritate him because he could see that what he was actually doing was his boss's job and to some extent his boss's boss's job without any kind of recognition. On the other hand, there were certain advantages to this informal arrangement. Even though he was working in a fairly bureaucratic organisation, he could suit himself whether or not he did it. He didn't have to deal with the paper work. Observes Durcan:

'What he had done was build a network. I suppose if people really were to be empowered they would have to build similar kinds of networks.'

It is generally believed that it is the new information technology that is making networking more widespread. Durcan feels the issue needs some clarification:

I think sometimes there's a risk of confusion. You have IT networks obviously which link all the micros and people do communicate. There are organisations that make an awful lot of use of electronic mail, which use the messages facilities to communicate very widely. Does it network? It don't think it does because most of the information you put on a screen like that is readable by a number of people.

It seems to me that networking really is a matter of informal

*relations. It's about having contact. Not that you always have to see
people face to face to make it work. You may have only had to see them
once face to face to make it work – telephone, fax, electronic networks
may work perfectly well after that, but there has to be some kind of
human contact. You can't just run it off machines. If you're really going
to be empowered then it's more than reading messages on screen.*

Savage identifies another worry about networking:

*There is some concern that the really effective networker bypasses all the
normal channels of authority. In one sense you can say wonderful,
because they actually get the job done, but in another sense you really
have to ask whether they get the short-term result on the basis of a long-
term problem?*

A Shadow Organisation

Sometimes networking can become the long-term solution. When I
worked for *International Management* magazine, I went to Jamaica to
write an article about a small telecommunications company that had
recently been nationalised. The Jamaican company had previously
been part of a very large UK electronics group and I asked the local
managing director who had now taken charge how he would
characterise the differences in the way the company now operated
compared to the time when it was controlled from the UK. His reply
was most unexpected.

He told me that there had been the normal pyramidal
organisation structure when his company was controlled from the
UK. But over the years an informal structure had grown up among
people in the company who got on well with each other and who
found that if they wanted to get things done they needed to contact
each other, not the people in the formal hierarchy. Largely unknown
to their UK masters, this informal network of control had ensured
that things ran smoothly.

When the Jamaican subsidiary was nationalised, a fresh look was
taken at how it might best be organised to take account of its new
ownership and circumstances. After some deliberation, it was

concluded that the former official organisation structure should be replaced by the informal shadow network that had operated so efficiently in the past. This was an example of networking taking over the whole organisation.

Networking is not quite so dominant in most organisations, but it is a force that cannot be ignored – and indeed many argue that it is something to be positively encouraged. The advance of networking as an informal way of doing business seems inevitable, throwing into question the traditional methods of delegation that rely on formal hierarchical structures.

OPEN MANAGEMENT

Networking can be expected to flourish in the open management culture that a growing number of companies are striving to create. Pat Hedges, head of internal communications and training at Parcel Force, defines open management as a culture where there is 'freedom of expression between the people who work in the organisations and those who manage it.' Hedges told *Director* magazine in April 1991 that 'open management can mean all you do is communicate very freely in all directions. Or it can mean that you put your money where your mouth is and pass a lot more responsibility, duty and accountability down the line to people'.

Corporate communications consultant John Smythe (co-author of *Corporate Reputation*, Century Business, 1992) of Smythe Dorward Lambert told the *Director*: 'When more information is made available there is absolutely no doubt that employees start taking more initiatives.'

In Chapter 11 a case study on Cow & Gate illustrates how one company is introducing an open management style to its organisation with the help of performance coaching.

GLOBALISATION – DECENTRALISATION AND MORE WIDELY DISPERSED AUTHORITY

The trend towards globalisation is putting enormous strains on conventional organisation structures. Every company of any reasonable size realises that in order to stay competitive it needs to expand its operations around the world. This inevitably means that authority is more widely dispersed. Senior executives of the parent company cannot physically be present in all the international locations where its subsidiaries are based. Modern technology is helping global companies to keep more in touch with their far-flung operations, but this is not the same as being on the spot reacting to local circumstances as they happen.

In the view of Dr Barry Brown, a consultant psychologist at the Independent Assessment & Research Centre, delegating in international organisations requires a high level of skill: 'The process of actually sharing the power has to be done very expertly and you have to be very comfortable with uncertainty.'

A study by Ashridge Management Research Group into the characteristics of a new breed of international manager has thrown up some encouraging discoveries, however. Notes Brown:

One of the characteristics is the acceptance of uncertainty – having a clear view about what needs to be achieved and not necessarily having to get it all right in every detail all the time and being able to allow people to make their best shot at something without interfering. You can't interfere, because you can't be in Zagreb and Paris and Madrid and Lisbon and Dublin all in one day. So the process has to be very well done.

The swing towards globalisation is reflected in the activities of those companies which service global production. Booz Allen & Hamilton, the major US consultancy, spent several years pursuing a policy of spreading its presence throughout the world in the belief that globalisation would eventually become the paramount issue for most of its clients. At times, the strategy led to substantial investment in parts of the world that showed little promise of a quick return.

Now, as the realisation has spread among its client firms that international expansion is the only real guarantee of survival, the consultancy is starting to reap rewards. John Harris, Booz Allen's European president, notes: 'Most of the companies we work for, even those in the Asia-Pacific region, are worried about world markets. They're worried about scale; they're worried about how they operate effectively in different cultures and how they use local people in companies that are owned in a different country.'

In order to respond to these concerns, Booz Allen has assembled international teams of consultants. 'The pan-European approach means doing European work with European teams,' explains Harris. 'We think that is the best way to serve clients who operate throughout Europe and the rest of the world. This is a major change because, historically, everyone consulting in Europe has been organised on a local basis.'

An important issue relating to globalisation is whether a company should centralise or decentralise. Brown of IARC says:

I can see increasing the use of technologically more advanced management information systems might encourage some companies to centralise rather than decentralise, but that hasn't universally been the response. It should give them more confidence to delegate. You've got more checks and you should be able to communicate more easily. Communication is a key issue here.

Some companies have seen the advance of modern telecommunications equipment and a slimmed down organisation as opportunities to concentrate control at the centre, but have then had second thoughts about the idea and reverted back to a decentralised structure. In a decentralised organisation delegation becomes an important consideration, because managers at the centre simply cannot be aware of all the developments in their far-flung corporate empire.

Savage argues that it is impossible to run decentralised organisations in the same mechanistic way as in the past:

Human beings are not very good at applying procedures in a mechanistic sense – and often you can't anyway. But if you have some set of principles that everyone can subscribe to, then those can be applied worldwide. The practice can be adapted to the country while hanging on to the principle. In the heyday of the Roman Empire you had a group of people who shared a set of principles as to what it was they were trying to achieve and how they should do it. Basically they went and applied that. It didn't matter where it was and they ran into problems later when that shared set of principles broke down.

One of the things successful global companies have in common is a set of principles – they have a certain way of doing things and they tend to apply that way of doing things everywhere they go, although the practice might differ from country to country.

Jim Durcan of Ashridge suggests that a distinction has to be drawn between decentralisation and delegation:

Delegation occurs when an individual manager decides to pass down some of his or her authority, some of the tasks with which they are charged, to someone else. Decentralisation is when an organisation takes a view about the kind of decisions that ought to be made at the centre or closer to the periphery. The globalisation issue is in a state of considerable flux.

There are those who believe that with the increased speed of modern communications it is sensible to run global organisations from the centre. This assumes that the information coming back from the far-flung regions of the organisation is accurate. There is nothing about the fact that it comes back faster that necessarily improves its accuracy. It just arrives more quickly. It can be wrong.

It doesn't necessarily mean either that the understanding at the centre of what is unfolding in the outside world is better than the understanding locally. The managers at the centre may still misunderstand the information they receive even if it is accurate.

To take a military analogy, the general at command headquarters can easily misunderstand information sent back to him from the battle front about movements on the part of the enemy. The message that comes back may indicate that the enemy is retreating, whereas in fact it is regrouping. The order goes out to surge forward. By the time the mistake is realised, the enemy may have regrouped with disastrous results for the army bearing down on it. The interpretation of what was going on might have been more accurate if it had been left to those closer to the scene of the action.

Questions about Convergence

In Durcan's experience, globalisation policies are often driven by marketeers 'who talk grandly in terms of global marketing and universal products.' The Ashridge leadership programme director is uneasy about this approach:

> I watch a world that in many ways is fragmenting. The Soviet Union has collapsed. Yugoslavia is in the process of tearing itself into smaller pieces. The EC's drive towards some kind of federal state appears to have stalled. It isn't clear that there is necessarily a kind of convergence.
> There was a lot of talk in the 1960s about the notion of convergence between societies through technological development. Technology was such a powerful influence on society it would increasingly be adopted universally and societies would converge. If you actually look at the way individual societies operate, it seems to me there is much less evidence of convergence. Are the Japanese any less Japanese than they were 50 years ago? I don't think so. They may have a veneer which Westerners may readily recognise, but it is far from clear that the Japanese are any less uniquely Japanese than they were.

If that is so, the whole concept of global products is open to question. The essence of the concept is that the same product or service can be sold anywhere in the world, preferably using the same marketing strategy. But if Durcan's observation about fragmentation is true there is a danger that the universal product actually fails to meet the needs of customers anywhere in the world.

A decentralised organisation, on the other hand, affords the opportunity for managers on the spot to make modifications to products to suit local needs and this can sometimes lead to a new range of products that might never have occurred to the managers at the centre of the organisation.

Decentralisation requires a new approach to delegation. Durcan points out:

> To decentralise you really have to replicate in the management hierarchy patterns of delegation. The people in the centre do have to be willing to let go with the national or regional subsidiaries. They have to have enough trust and confidence to believe in the people running those operations actually to let go. Even better, they might see it as an opportunity to develop them.

Globalisation, also emphasizes that increased competition and the rapid pace of change all put pressures on organisations in terms of their ability to be flexible and responsive to market conditions:

> I think the more those pressures increase, the more the pressures for decentralisation and delegation grow, particularly for firms which have relatively complex product structures. If you're only selling one product then maybe you can take all the decisions at the centre. If you're dealing with 30,000 customers and you're dealing with 500 products, you can't. It's going to have to be substantially delegated. There's a lot of scope around for delegation and there's a lot of pressure on organisations to do it.

Better educated workforce – higher expectations from the job

There is also considerable pressure from the workforce for more widespread delegation. The UK is not alone in seeing an ever higher proportion of graduates entering its workforce. A more intelligent workforce almost certainly means that there are more employees who are unprepared simply to do what they are told, and who want the freedom to take initiatives.

There is a view that the enormous growth in numbers of the self-employed over the past decade is partly a reaction by people who were becoming increasingly disenchanted with working for organisations that simply hand down instructions and leave no room for personal initiatives.

Yet Durcan of Ashridge has found little evidence that UK companies are taking account of this shift in employee attitude:

> *If you listen to what employees say about their managers they complain that they are not stretched, not grown and not improved. So they move on. Often they move because the job they're offered involves more money, but they are also looking for jobs which will give them more scope.*

LESS JOB SECURITY

In the past employees often endured autocratic organisations because they enjoyed job security. That is no longer true. The recession and the drive to make organisations leaner and more competitive has put paid to job security, and without it employees naturally look for other compensations. They are less likely to be tolerant of organisations that tie them down to rigid procedures and discourage individual initiatives. Observes Durcan:

> *If we've learned anything from the 1980s it's that there is no longer any job security. But if there is no job security what is the point of a job? Maybe in that case people raise their sights to what the job ought to offer them. Previously they may have accepted being told what to do as the price of security, but if they're not getting security out of it, why should they accept being told what to do?*

Less awe of authority

In general, there is less awe of authority today than in past generations. Parental control has gradually been eroded since Victorian times and there is evidence of much less respect for authority in schools and other institutions. There are growing signs that royalty is no longer looked up to in the way that it was.

Of course, the young have always rebelled against authority as a means of self-expression and as a way of affirming a right to their own culture. The fashion fads that periodically sweep through the younger generation and the mania for certain kinds of popular music all underline a desire to establish their own identity and escape the rules and norms of adult society.

In the world at large, we have witnessed in recent years the fall of one despotic regime after another in Eastern Europe. People power has taken over from tyranny. While in the more affluent nations of the West, the urge to rebel and be assertive may not be quite so strong, there is no doubt that the acceptance of authority is no longer automatic. People want a greater say in their own future and they want the freedom to act according to their own judgements.

This trend has some unfortunate repercussions. Police forces all over Britain are struggling to maintain the rule of law, which is an essential ingredient of democracy. But anarchy has its positive aspects as well. When people feel they have the freedom to express themselves, they make a far more valuable contribution to society than if they are merely cogs in an established machine. Those in a position to delegate would be foolish not to recognise the opportunity that this trend opens up to channel the talents of people at all levels of the organisation for mutual benefit.

Leadership vacuum

Effective delegation requires skilled leaders, but Warren Bennis, who has written several books on the subject, has been alerting the world to the dire consequences of an apparently universal leadership vacuum. Bennis attributes the dearth of leaders in the US to the decline of the US economy relative to other industrial nations, though he sees the same lack of decisive leadership in the rest of the world.

He wonders whether some of the new leaders of Eastern Europe are pointing the way to future developments which may turn conventional wisdom about leadership on its head. He points out that poets, journalists and playwrights are emerging as leaders. 'But they too are having their problems and I think they will get worse,' he reflected when I questioned him on the subject, adding as an afterthought: 'Is there any leader now not in trouble?'

Orthodox perceptions of leadership could also be changed by the growth in the US and the UK of small business entrepreneurs, by definition leaders of the firms they found. In Bennis's words:

There may be a dispersion of leadership to more self-managed businesses. That means more leadership not less, and this is where the growth is coming from. In the US, it is not the Fortune 500 *that are the growing industries; it's the firms with 50 to 250 employees where the growth has been.*

Bennis' own baptism of fire as a leader came during a seven-year spell as president of the University of Cincinnati in the 1970s. It was a time of anarchic student unrest and distrust of authority. It was also a time of multiple minority interests and Bennis found himself besieged by the conflicting demands of a plethora of university interest groups. He admits: 'It was a tough time for me, because the truth is I didn't feel at all successful as a leader.'

For his book, *On Becoming a Leader*, Bennis interviewed 29 American leaders from various walks of life and arrived at some universal conclusions about the nature of leadership. One is that leaders are not born; they are made. Yet Bennis decries most of the attempts to teach leadership:

I say in the book that MA, PhD and MBA are not the important letters after your name; the important letters are JOB. Having said that I still think leadership can be taught, but I don't think we are very knowledgeable yet about how to teach it. Most good business schools don't teach leadership; they teach management. They teach certain quantifiable skills to a recipe. The idea of the one-minute manager is an appalling concept to me because it seems to grow out of the fast-food era. It implies that if you pop someone into the micro oven, out pops a McLeader.

It is something of a paradox that in the view of people like Bennis there is a universal decline in leadership skills just when there are all kinds of pressures on the people who run organisations to excel at being good delegators. Perhaps a more positive way to look at it is that new organisation structures, less autocratic control, and greater expectations by employees will encourage leaders to delegate with more skill. Their own role as leaders might be diminishing, but that could partly be because they are passing more responsibility down the line to a more empowered workforce that is anxious to perform tasks that give them more job satisfaction. Maybe most people want to be a mini-leader in their own right. Certainly, delegation at its best is a way to put them in charge of their own destinies.

THE ORGANISATION OF THE FUTURE

In the mid-1980s there was much debate about the return of the macho manager who was re-asserting his power and control in the wake of waning union influence. The pendulum seems to be swinging back in the opposite direction at the beginning of the 1990s. Empowerment is ushering in an era in which conflict and confrontation give way to co-operation and collaborative effort and in which the talents of all the work force are harnessed for the benefit of the organisation as a whole.

This trend was summed up graphically by Graham Prentice, a Nestles personnel manager, in an article in *Personnel Management* magazine:

I believe the successful management style of the future will be one which is strongly focused on behavioural characteristics. This means managers who value quality and prefer openness, who will share goals with subordinates, be concerned about others, supportive, good listeners, receptive to suggestions, and who communicate easily. In businesses, we tend to be competitive, action-oriented and autonomous, and to think analytically, concretely and rationally. In managing in a more behavioural way, managers will need to be more 'nurturing', which perhaps is not automatically regarded as a business-oriented characteristic.

Prentice predicted that networking will become more common. He foresaw networkers leaving the central organisation and selling back services to the parent company, but remaining in close contact with the parent by receiving training and support. Prentice went on:

In the future organisations will not be managed by command, but by persuasion and consent. Management style will need to be open and democratic; shared problem-solving will be the key. Managing will be concerned with developing other people's capacity to handle problems. The culture of consent will not have authority bound in the job; rather the style will be based on persuasion and continual encouragement.

4. Empowerment

One of today's most hotly debated issues in enlightened management circles is the concept of *empowerment*. Some management experts see it as the magic formula that will unleash the latent talents of the workforce and lead to previously unimagined leaps in efficiency and productivity. Empowerment, as far as delegation is concerned, essentially means enabling employees to take personal initiatives beyond the scope of their normal work but within a set of company values. This presupposes that a company's employees are all aware of what those values are and how they apply to the different kinds of devolved responsibility that may be passed down to them. It also assumes that employees are capable of taking personal initiatives and indeed are motivated to do so. Some management thinkers are convinced that there is a wide group of people in any organisation who are perfectly happy to do mundane jobs. They reserve their energies and their creativity for social activities outside the company gate.

However, as was pointed out in the previous chapter, there are an enormous number of developments in the corporate world that are making it essential to delegate more widely and to delegate more worthwhile work that enriches subordinates and helps them to grow in their job. The trend now is to delegate results rather than tasks. This means that employees at all levels will be called upon to take more personal initiatives and senior managers will need to give up more control and entrust more to those they lead.

In his book *Why Leaders Can't Lead*, Warren Bennis describes empowerment as the 'collective effect of leadership'. He suggests that in organisations with effective leaders, empowerment is most evident in four themes:

- *People feel significant.* Everyone feels that he or she makes a difference to the success of the organisation.
- *Learning and competence matter.* Leaders value learning and mastery, and so do people who work for leaders. Leaders make it clear that there is no failure, only mistakes that give us feedback and tell us what to do next.
- *People are part of a community.* Where there is leadership, there is a team, a family, a unity. Even people who do not especially like each other feel a sense of community.
- *Work is exciting.* Where there are leaders, work is stimulating, challenging, fascinating and fun. An essential ingredient in organisation leadership is pulling rather than pushing people toward a goal. A 'pull' style of influence attracts and energises people to enrol in an exciting vision of the future. It motivates through identification, rather than through rewards and punishments.

Everyone Matters

Adrian Savage, of Assessment Design Services, the Leamington Spa management training agency, sees empowerment in a similar light. He sums it up as 'allowing people to feel that their job matters. I would put it as baldly as that.' He questions the definition of empowerment that says it is purely about pushing decisions down the line, because, in his view, a lot of subordinates are not prepared to take on the extra responsibility that decision-making demands. 'In some cases,' he adds, 'they are not able to take decisions; they don't have the information. But I think what is important is that they feel whatever they do matters – even if it is only cleaning the floor in the foyer. If we think our work doesn't matter then, at best, we simply do it for money – also it's a very small step to thinking we don't matter.'

In Savage's view empowerment is moving away from the notion of 'getting the ideas out of the heads of the managers into the hands of the workers – the idea that your position in the hierarchy of the organisation tells you the extent to which you're allowed to think and that if you're at the bottom of the hierarchy it isn't very often and it isn't very much. You just do.'

MANAGING INSTABILITY

Savage argues that empowerment and devolved responsibility have now become vital ingredients for any organisation that is intent on being flexible and fast reacting to the rapid changes in today's unstable business climate:

> *Most of our experience of running organisations has been in conditions of considerable stability – social stability, financial stability, market stability – where if you were the only carpenter in a village and people wanted something done in wood they came to you. We are not in a stable environment any more.*
>
> *Most of our traditional methodologies for managing are still geared to stability; we don't have it any more. Empowerment is a way of asking: how do we cope in a situation where we cannot operate according to a hierarchical chain of command? One approach is that you de-skill all possible jobs. You have one person sitting somewhere taking all the decisions – every decision is directed to that person; everyone else is just doing things. Not very feasible, but some organisations try to run like that – what Handy [Charles Handy, the management expert] calls the* spider's web. *Or you try to push some of the decision-making, some of that ability to take action without reference to other people, out to the periphery.*

Competing with the Japanese

The concept of empowerment grew out of the desire among American corporations to find a way to compete more effectively with the Japanese. The Americans have looked at the way Japanese firms operate and tried to understand what it is that makes them so much more productive and successful. The common western stereotype of the way a Japanese organisation operates is that there is plenty of consultation and involvement of the work force. Toyota, the Japanese car maker, is a good example. In the mid-1960s Toyota was receiving something like 80,000 suggestions a year from its employees, 80 per cent of which were implemented. Today, the Japanese car maker gets two million suggestions a year and implements 97 per cent of them.

A suggestion might be as minor as an employee requesting to move his desk two feet in another direction to make it easier to work. The supervisor gives the go-ahead, but it turns out that there is no improvement after all. The employee asks permission to move the desk back again. That is counted as two implemented suggestions!

This does not sound like the sort of action that is going to make Toyota more competitive than any other car company in the world. But the point is that with two million suggestions being made every year, it only requires one per cent of them to have any significance to make a major impact on the way the company performs. But perhaps more importantly, Toyota has created the kind of culture that is geared to the notion that everyone in the organisation can bring about change. If someone suggests a change the automatic response is go ahead. Unlike most UK and US corporations, Japanese companies encourage their employees to experiment, however doubtful the benefit might seem on the surface.

In the UK, the attitude is more likely to be: 'What's the evidence for that?' Or: 'We tried that five years ago and it didn't work.' We look for reasons for failure rather than experiment on the basis that something worthwhile might emerge from change.

Stephen Taylor, chairman of London-based management consultants Kinsley Lord, observes:

> In Japan if an idea is proposed people look for what's good in it rather than what's unacceptable. It's something to do with the administrative culture of Britain that basically wants to retain the status quo. It's a lot easier to say no than to say yes. When you say no, it's the end of the story. If you say yes, it might be a bad idea, in which case you're going to get into trouble. Secondly, you've got to do some work to make it happen. So it's a lot easier to reject than to accept.

Anyone with even the vaguest notion of what has been happening on the world scene will have noticed that the Japanese approach is the one that has been delivering the best results. The problem for the West, however, is that there is no escaping that the

Japanese culture is alien to our way of life. The American culture, for example, is based on the individual – the archetypal American hero is the lone cowboy who goes out to fight the Indians. Everything depends on him, whereas in Eastern cultures the individual is subordinated to the collective effort. Teamwork and unselfish dedication owe more to Eastern culture than they do to any particular management technique or tool.

Japanese employees are probably not motivated in the same way as Western employees either. Tony Knight of Henley Management College points out that Japanese workers can afford to be more altruistic than Western employees because they generally operate under a policy of life-long employment with one company:

I suspect Japanese people are less concerned about promotion prospects because they are based largely on age and length of service, whereas in this country it would be very difficult to persuade workers that they should work harder for the good of the company. They would be looking to gain practical advantage – promotion, or extra training, expertise or pay.

However, that does not mean that lessons cannot be learned from the Japanese success story. It might be impossible to replicate the Eastern culture in the West, but much can be gained from extracting certain elements of that culture and adapting them to the Western way of life. In their search for the key ingredients of the Japanese model, the Americans have concluded that empowerment is an important element in the desire to achieve greater productivity from the workforce. According to Jim Durcan:

They looked at the way US auto factories, for example, were run compared to Japanese auto factories. The US auto factories had been heavily influenced by Taylorian models and by union conflicts into becoming tightly circumscribed jobs, fixed procedures, absolutely nothing in terms of flexible working, multi-skilling, employee responsiveness – any of those sorts of things – and they took a look at the Japanese cost patterns and thought that American industry was just going down the plug. So they began to think that perhaps what they needed to do was to unlock the talent in the American workforce in the way that the Japanese seem to. I think that takes you around eventually to empowerment.'

Productivity Gains

Research carried out by Quinn Mills, a US management expert, has led him to the conclusion that the empowered organisation that unleashes the creativity of its work force can routinely achieve productivity gains of between 30 per cent and 50 per cent in a year. Nuclear Electric's Hartlepool power station is expecting to achieve a 30 per cent increase in output as a result of introducing empowerment.

Stephen Taylor of management consultants Kinsley Lord, who are advising Nuclear Electric, says:

There has to be a business objective rather than simply regarding empowerment and delegation as a good idea. It is increasingly hard to differentiate yourself in the market-place through the products and services that you offer because they are easy to ape. Brand names are still a good differentiator, but in the long run what you want is an organisation that uses its people to better effect because that's really the only asset an organisation has. Unfortunately most organisations use their people rather badly.

In 1991 Kinsley Lord undertook a survey of quarter of a million people working in the National Health Service in Britain, possibly the most comprehensive inquiry of its kind ever undertaken anywhere in the world. The conclusion was that the NHS, which has always tended to attribute most of its ills to lack of resources, could make enormous productivity gains if its employees were 'properly managed and properly developed'. Such findings prompt Stephen Taylor to declare that the impact of empowerment is 'potentially quite phenomenal'.

Instances abound of empowerment's potent force for beneficial change. British Airways' engineering division, for example, set some cost saving targets to reduce overheads. Normally this would have been achieved by mandatory budget cuts. But by seeking suggestions from front-line staff – maintenance and overhaul engineers – they came up with savings that were three times greater than those targeted.

Taking Initiatives

The trend towards empowerment has brought about a re-examination of the benefits of delegation and caused it to be seen in a new light. Traditionally, with delegation, a manager says to his subordinate: 'I want you to deal with this task, here are the limits of your authority, work within these tightly prescribed constraints'. A good delegator will also say: 'Just outline for me how you intend to tackle this' with the intention of achieving a piece of positive coaching and ensuring the subordinate is unlikely to run off the rails. But all the initiation is coming from the manager. The manager initiates the delegating process. The manager initiates the reporting process and any kind of review process.

With empowerment, on the other hand, an attempt is being made to change the way subordinates view their job so that they are more willing to take initiatives. The initiative may simply be going to your manager and saying: 'You are clearly very busy with Y account, why don't you let me tackle X account?' It may be individuals taking responsibility upon themselves to deal with things without any referral to their manager. Delegation is actioned by the manager. Empowerment, if it works well, is actioned by the subordinate.

Adds Stephen Taylor of Kinsley Lord:

It's not that you have an unempowered organisation where there are lots of rules and an empowered organisation where there aren't any rules. That isn't the distinction we are talking about. We are talking about people being guided in their behaviour not by a manual of procedure, but by an understanding of why those procedures are there. In other words, the conduct is framed within the values and the business purpose of the organisation.

Empowerment Sceptics

Not everyone is convinced that empowerment is going to lead the way to a new era of enlightenment, however. Bernard Taylor, professor of business policy at Henley Management College, is highly sceptical:

> *When I hear the word empowerment, I reach for my gun, because it's one of those cloudy words. It's like new bottles for old wine. I like delegation because it's a clean word. Empowerment is a rather dirty word and I am suspicious of it because it doesn't exist as a word. It's something somebody coined in Minnesota or somewhere.*

Tony Knight, director of the strategic management programme at Henley Management College, stresses that empowerment should not be allowed to become abdication of responsibility; it is vital that the parameters within which employees can take personal initiatives are clearly spelled out:

> *It would be totally irresponsible to devolve such levels of authority you are abdicating all responsibility and saying get on with it. You've got to know what authority has been devolved and the limits of that authority. It's fine for people to feel that they can solve customers' problems or deal with situations within certain defined limits, but they have also got to feel confident that they can get advice, guidance and information from higher up.*

Dr Paul Taffinder, a management consultant with Coopers Deloitte who specialises in organisational change in the financial services sector, contends that empowerment wrongly applied can cause a lot of tension.

> *You achieve a company's purpose in part by everyone knowing what their role is and what value they add, but ultimately you need some mechanism to give the organisation a sense of direction. It leads to tension if you have total empowerment without some form of authority on which people can act. The chief executive is ultimately responsible for*

achieving earnings per share, for example, over a period of years. He needs to know month by month how he is doing in order to achieve that objective and he needs to be able to take effective action if he is not achieving the objective. In an empowered organisation, effective action might be quite different from that taken in a controlled organisation, but ultimately it is necessary to provide the chief executive with information about performance.

Sheila Rothwell points out that there is a danger that empowerment

can be exploitation. You are just pushing off all the things in your job description you don't like doing on to somebody else, saying that they are enriched and empowered. In terms of structuring, it is very much a question of trying to draw the line between responsibility and accountability. The person at the top still retains the accountability, but you can delegate the responsibility for doing something. The unions will still object to that because they're still going to be blamed if they do something that doesn't work even if the person at the top is also blamed for it.

Durcan has serious doubts about whether organisations are capable of empowering employees:

My difficulty is with the notion that organisations empower people. I know that organisations can disempower people, if that's a word. You can create an organisation culture that says never take any chances, always cover your back, always put it in writing, always make sure you've got authority, always get them to sign it before you do it, it doesn't matter if it works as long as you've got a signature on a piece of paper. All of those things are depowering people.

With empowerment I think you can create organisational cultures which make it easier to delegate, but to some extent it must come from the subordinates as well. I can see how a manager can turn to a subordinate and tell him 'I'm going to delegate this to you'. Can a manager turn to a subordinate in the same way and say 'I'm going to empower you to do this'? No he can't, because that's about their display of initiative.

Durcan's doubts are borne out by the experience of Alastair Wright, human resource director of Digital Equipment Corp.'s UK subsidiary:

> *It took me a long time to learn a fundamental truth about empowerment: you cannot give empowerment. People themselves have to be in a position to want to do things. I used to think you could just sprinkle golden dust on their head and say: 'Now you're empowered. Go away and multiply'. It doesn't work because they don't do it. They are so constrained by the existing paradigm.*

More than MbO

To some extent Management by Objectives (MbO), a popular technique in the 1970s, was meant to tackle this problem. The boss and his subordinate set goals and performance measurements together. The extent of a subordinate's span of authority was mutually agreed with his boss. But Durcan believes that empowerment goes much further:

> *MbO, is seems to me, largely assumes that when you have the crucial meeting (between boss and subordinate) you know where you're going. The important thing about empowerment is that it is equipping employees to handle a situation even when they don't know where they're going.*

More recently, MbO has been superseded by performance management, a technique that similarly involves setting objectives with subordinates and teams, monitoring progress, feeding back results and coaching and counselling. 'Since with performance management, development of the subordinate is explicitly on the manager's agenda, you are more likely to find task allocation based on development and performance,' observes Michael Thomas, director of organisation and quality at PA Management Consultants.

According to Alan Fowler, a personnel consultant, the starting point of a full-blown performance management system (PMS) is a definition of the organisation's mission, aims and values – a culture feature not found in MbO. Writing in *Personnel Management* magazine, Fowler adds:

> *Corporate and divisional objectives are then identified which reflect or support the corporate mission. The objectives of individual managers and their support staff are evolved similarly as part of a cascade of integrated goal and standard setting. Unlike MbO, which was generally limited in application to managers, PMS schemes are being extended to all staff. The whole process is more cohesive and strategically focused than MbO – and consequently stands a better chance of success.*

Fowler also points out that there is recognition that peformance cannot be assessed purely by quantified measurement. Qualitative performance indicators are given full recognition, for example, by the use of customer attitude and opinion surveys.

Examples of Empowerment

A simple example of empowerment is where a disgruntled customer telephones a company at lunchtime to complain about an order that has failed to arrive. The manager responsible is not available: he is attending a business lunch and is unlikely to return until late afternoon (possibly the worse for wear). The customer threatens to cancel the order unless it is dispatched immediately. The receptionist who takes the call promises to pursue the matter, gets on to warehousing, sorts the order out and has it dispatched by courier before the manager gets back from lunch.

For the receptionist to feel confident about taking this initiative, she needs to have established some kind of informal network that ignores the formal reporting relationships. She needs a good informal relationship with the people in the warehouse and the people who operate the delivery service. Otherwise when she contacts them they are unlikely to be very co-operative. If she knows them well, has been in contact with them before, and particularly if they have all been applauded for similar enterprise, she will have no difficulty in getting them to take such swift action.

Many people in many organisations would probably feel uneasy about taking that kind of initiative. A lot of people would convince themselves that it did not lie within their job description. As Frederick Herzberg, the celebrated US behavioural scientist, has pointed out, plenty of people are quite happy to do mundane jobs and are unlikely to want extra responsibility. But there is ample evidence to suggest that if empowered to do so, many employees would welcome the opportunity to expand the narrow scope of their routine work and take initiatives that benefit both them and their organisation.

A growing number of organisations are recognising that empowerment can provide the key for involving employees down the line in solving problems that traditionally would have been the province of top management. For many years Boots the Chemists, for example, found that similar stores could have turnover levels varying by 15 per cent or more. The company concluded that the difference was entirely attributable to the respective abilities of the store managers to motivate their staff. To tackle the problem, Boots is involving sales assistants in the front line in defining their own roles and developing their skills and contribution. Teams of staff in stores now regularly meet together to plan and implement better ways of further improving their store performance.

Wylfa Power Station in Anglesey, part of Nuclear Electric, has traditionally had to close one of its reactors eight weeks of the year for maintenance. The cost is £2.5 million a week in lost electricity production. In 1991 staff at all levels of the power station worked together to find a way to reduce the downtime. The complexity of such a change in a nuclear power station, with its stringent safety requirements, is immense. But the teams identified new procedures, new ways of working together and new skills which are expected to result in annual revenue gains of some £4 million.

Similarly, Esso Petroleum set up teams representing officers, ratings and support staff to redesign working patterns when the crews of its giant oil tankers were drastically reduced from 30 to 19 in 1990 – a feat that was initially regarded as impossible.

At Royal Liverpool Children's Hospital, nurses in the accident and emergency department were distressed by the suffering of children who had to wait up to two hours to see a doctor. They knew that the problem was not simply staff numbers. With the co-operation of doctors, the nurses plotted the type and timing of all admissions. Patterns emerged. They saw that peaks and troughs could be radically reduced by small changes in working hours, staggered meal breaks and a new admissions procedure. They set themselves the goal that no child would be kept waiting more than 30 minutes. In 1991 they achieved that goal for 99 per cent of admissions.

These are four very different organisations: a leading high street retailing group; a high technology utility progressively losing its state subsidy; an American-owned oil major; and the NHS in the public sector. Yet, in all of them, teams of people came together to reshape how they worked in order to do things better, faster and more cheaply.

Continuous Improvement

Management consultants Kinsley Lord have made a study of the empowered organisation to understand more fully its potential for enlightened change. Stephen Taylor explains that:

> Its essence is that it is able to improve continuously, not just in response to a major challenge or crisis. It does so by adapting itself in big and little ways, every day at all levels, feeding the learning from its experience back into how it works. Its secret is that it makes much more powerful use than does the 'command' organisation of the abilities and enthusiasm of its people.

The End of the Command Organisation

The London consultants have identified three main reasons why the empowered organisation can be expected to replace the command organisation:

1. The command organisation's decision-making is too centralised, so it changes itself less quickly and less effectively than the organisation which not merely permits, but expects, continuing

innovation. For example, the command organisation assumes that top management understands the customer better than front-line employees, when the reverse is the case.

2. It ignores rather than cherishes the abilities of its staff, so its costs are too high. It believes that capital investment, new technology and information systems are the best ways to raise productivity. In fact experience shows that 'working smarter' has always generated the meteoric improvements. Time and again, attitude surveys in large organisations show the frustration of employees who know they can contribute far more than they are asked to.

3. The command organisation increasingly fails to attract able people, those who want a job that has meaning beyond earning a living, who demand freedom in the way they work, and who expect roles in which they will learn and grow. They do not want to be a part of organisations which allow them less initiatives in their paid employment than they use in running their lives, or who expect them to leave their brains in the locker room when they come to work.

Tapping Talents

There is an abundance of evidence that suggests that employees in mundane jobs are capable of being stretched. Management guru Tom Peters cites the example of an American sausage factory. Ten workers performing the most menial of tasks were picked at random from the processing line. All but two of them were leading private lives that were full of achievement. Two of them had built their own homes. One was a leading light opera singer in the local community. Another ran a youth group.

Peters asked the valid question: why was it that employees appear to leave their talents at the factory gate when they come to work? The simple answer is because organisations have never tapped those talents and the workers have grown accustomed to working within tightly prescribed limits.

Durcan has had similar experiences. He lives in Oxford and over the years has come to know quite a few car factory workers:

In private life you find them turning up as local councillors; you find them running allotments, local football teams and Boy Scouts' groups. These are all activities that require management skills. The difficulty for firms like Rover is how to tap some of that. There are those who have a fairly low drive for independence and achievement and for wanting to take initiatives and responsibility.

One study has shown that in 90 per cent of manual jobs in the UK, the shopfloor operative uses more skill driving to work than at any time during the working day.

At a recent London seminar attended by 250 senior executives paying £400 a head for the privilege, Tom Peters asked a rhetorical, but deliberately provocative question:

What do you and your colleagues as managers see – really see – when you look in the eye of a first-line employee? Do you see a ne'er-do-well beneath the span of control of one to six which is present in your company, who rips you off if you turn your back for more than 30 or 40 nano-seconds, who requires a 500-page policy manual that tells him when to go to the bathroom? Or do you see a person who can literally fly to the moon without a face mask if only you would train the hell out of them, get the hell out of their way and give them something worth doing?

Peters sums up the attitude of Western managers towards first-line workers with a conclusion he has reached from analysis of British and American annual reports. Company officers in Britain and the USA, he observes, are apparently born with names, but workers aren't. Peters arrived at this observation by noting that you can always find the names of managers in the captions underneath pictures in annual reports but you can hardly ever find the names of employees under their photographs. Maintains Peters:

It is demeaning to the human being. A car is a great car, an aircraft engine is a great aircraft engine, to the extent that the person working on the front line gives a damn and is committed. It's virtually as simple as that.

Entrenched Attitudes

Wright of Digital Equipment also believes that entrenched attitudes about the differences between the capabilities of managers and the rest of the work force have to be overcome before empowerment can catch hold:

> If you ask people to describe the paradigm of leadership/management, you get some very interesting feedback. It's all about leaders being superhuman. They are usually male, macho, they never show their emotions, they can never be wrong. If you ask the same question about the paradigm of followership, they do what they are told, they usually whinge and complain, they tend to be the lower classes, they have no ambition.

This view is in stark contrast to what Wright sees as the empowered employee:

> No matter what happens to the world outside them they are in control. They make the choices. That to me is the definition of an empowered person, whereas most people have not been brought up like that. They've been brought up to do what they are told. They aren't encouraged to question things, to express themselves, to be creative, to try things out, to learn, to step outside of the model and do things differently.

There is a widely-used phrase at Digital: 'It is easier to seek forgiveness than to seek authority.' But Wright believes there will have to be some fundamental shifts before the full scope of empowerment can be embraced by the majority of the work force:

> We've discovered that self-esteem is very important in this process. People have to have a very high self-image. They have to understand themselves first of all, because you can't have self-esteem if you don't understand what's happening inside you. You have to help them raise their self-esteem; then you have to coach them through the process.

Demotivated

Peters' research leads him to believe that the average shopfloor worker in Britain and the US is very demotivated. He predicts, however, that this will have to change with the new flatter organisation structures that are being implemented by the most successful companies. 'In the three layer organisation the average person on the front line – real front line, clerk, sweeper – has to be a strategically-oriented, totally empowered person.'

He cites the example of the Harley Davidson motorcycle factory in the US, which came close to being put out of business by Japanese competition in the 1970s. The company has since made a remarkable comeback and Peters puts it all down to the decision by top management to 'unlock the power of the workforce.'

Harley Davidson is now organised into semi-autonomous work teams rather than undifferentiated assembly lines. Previously the plant boasted 27 production controllers and nothing ever went out on time. It now has one production controller and everything goes out on deadline. Peters argues that it is

> *common sense to listen to the people who are closest to the problem, although it is not the British or American tradition . . . The British manager's instinct and the American manager's instinct is not to fix the problem with training. It's to fix the problem by throwing more automation at it – let's dump 20 robots on the scene and see what happens; let's hire 25 MBAs and get them sitting down in front of their computer screens and so on. It's not our instinct to look at our workforce for constant and perpetual improvement in pursuit of world class quality or costs or whatever your competitive variable may be.*

Parent and Child

Part of the problem is that employees have long grown accustomed to the idea that they are not supposed to take initiatives. They have become used, in terms of Transactional Analysis, to playing the role of the child to the parent. They see themselves as the obedient child and do what they are told. What they do outside the work place is quite another matter. Ashridge's Durcan believes that:

> *Managers who engage in parental kind of behaviour attract over time subordinates who want to behave like children. There's a kind of symmetry there, which is what is so difficult for managers when they take up new posts. They don't know what the expectations of the followers are. If the subordinates have been used to being treated as children by management and the new boss arrives wanting to encourage adult status for all, nobody wants to play that game. It's boring.*

The tide may be turning, however. Thomas of PA Management Consultants points out that UK companies are increasingly tightening up their recruitment policies and exploring new employees' motivational attitudes as well as their career records. He predicts that companies will steadily build up a core cadre of employees who will expect to be empowered and given the opportunity to take initiatives outside the limited scope of their jobs. Thomas expects this development to happen more quickly in some sectors of business than others. It is more evident in modern engineering companies where the number of people employed is quite low and the job content reasonably high. In such organisations the emphasis is on skilling up.

De-Skilling

It is also more apparent in professional organisations which have always tended to have loose-knit structures. In other sectors such as food retailing the trend is towards de-skilling in favour of hi-tech. In such companies there is 'a work system which accepts and thrives, in one sense, on very low levels of skill in the workforce, very high levels of employee turnover and low levels of pay,' in Thomas's view. 'It's a management strategy to put huge amounts of investment in point-of-sale technology and no investment in people.' In such organisations, it is hard to see empowerment gaining hold in the foreseeable future.

Michael Stanton, a management consultant with Coopers Deloitte who specialises in organisational change, takes issue with this view, however. 'I would argue that every job is empowerable to some extent.' Stanton points out that simplified check-out procedures at supermarkets, in fact leave the staff more free to talk to customers and explore their needs. He also observes that check-out staff in many supermarket chains are being empowered to take more high level decisions. They are being given the authority to approve cheques up to a certain amount, for example, without reference to a supervisor.

Taffinder of Cooper Deloitte argues that to some extent de-skilling helps to further the cause of empowerment. He suggests that one of the barriers to empowerment and delegation has been organisations that are too ambiguous in their aims.

People haven't really known very clearly what the organisation expects of them. You have had people in banking, for example, trying to sell 200 different products without being trained to understand those products. To some extent de-skilling goes with empowerment. The job scope is being better defined. People are being given the conditions in which they are able to do the job to a very high standard; they're much more clear about their linkages to their suppliers and their customers.

In this case, you can empower and say: 'Those are the parameters you have to play with. It's up to you how you actually optimise that.' There's a much more defined situation. Providing empowerment in an over-complex situation where you're not providing some ground rules and guidance to people is really a recipe for disaster.

Looking for volunteers

The problem as Dr Barry Brown of The Independent Assessment & Research Centre in London sees it, is trying to identify those employees who are keen to become empowered and those who would prefer to remain within the confines of routine jobs. Current methods of management assessment tend to imply that there are certain people who naturally seek empowerment and those who don't, but Brown suggests it could be more complicated than that:

Supposing it is the case that actually everybody is potentially capable of engaging in the process of empowerment. It's just that some people have more practice than others and are working in an environment where they are given more opportunity than others. It could be that people are not infinitely plastic but more plastic than they are given credit for. Or it could be some people are more plastic than others. But I don't think you can assume that a lowly employee who is not skilled and is doing a routine repetitive job is inherently less able to take part in a delegation process.

A Shoal of Fish

Consultants Kinsley Lord point out that the empowered organisation is held together by forces that are different from those which bind the command organisation. If the conventional metaphor for the command organisation is a dinosaur with the brain at the top issuing instructions to the ponderous body, then the empowered organisation might be compared to a shoal of fish, moving rapidly and constantly adjusting its shape through signals that are instantly understood.

Jim Durcan believes that empowerment is the key to unlocking subordinates' untapped energies:

I have never found a manager who will honestly say he gets 100 per cent out of the people who work for him, not just in terms of performance, but on the much more challenging criterion of whether you actually use 100 per cent of their talent and energy. Most managers believe they are lucky if they get half of it. If, however, you get empowerment right you can achieve a high measure because the subordinates deliver their own energy and they deliver their own talents appropriate to the needs of the situation. The more they do the more they will find they are able to do.

The problem is that with any given organisation there are always powerful forces which hold it where it is – like the expectations of all the people in the organisation. At its best, empowerment taps people's energies and talents, but any organisation not previously strong in those kinds of areas that suddenly announces it is sold on empowerment underestimates the complexity of handling that as a piece of organisational change.

If the organisation previously has largely been a tell'em organisation where managers are used to adopting a fairly authoritarian manner and are used to driving things forward – used, in TA terms, to behaving as parents – first of all you've got to persuade the managers about the benefits of behaving differently. You have to coach them to the point where they behave differently. If they have had 30 to 40 years' practice of behaving in this way you have got an enormous amount of unlearning before you do any learning, if they're actually going to acquire new habits.

Even when that change has been achieved, there are still all the procedures and systems in the organisation which previously served to reinforce the message about 'do as you're told', including probably disciplinary systems, reward systems and appraisal systems. All those need to be unscrambled and put back together again. Then the expectations of all the people in the organisation who have been used to working for this telling organisation have to be dealt with. Adds Durcan:

For an existing organisation to make a fundamental change like that, it's an enormous upheaval. In many ways you could argue that you've got the wrong people both as managers and followers for that kind of behaviour and you've got an organisation which is shaped to deliver the kind of behaviour you no longer want.

Where are the Guidelines?
One of the problems is that there cannot be precise guidelines for empowerment. They are practically a contradiction in terms. If you attach a set of rules to empowerment you are back talking about Management by Objectives or outmoded forms of delegation. Consultants Kinsley Lord comment:

While the classic command business is withering in Britain, the empowered organisation is still far from established. It is hard to understand the empowered organisation from the perspective of the command model. If there are few rules, what stops people doing what they shouldn't? How can there be the necessary discipline, control and probity? How can people be allowed to do things in different ways where, say, the safety requirements of an oil refinery, the operational independence of parts of an airline, the consistency of presentation of a retailer or the quality of treatment expected from a government department demand that standards are set and enforced?

The key is that people must understand not merely the rules, but the purpose behind them. Then rules are no longer rules but best practice, gladly embraced and improved daily by the valued experience of those who operate them. A successful franchise business illustrates this. The franchisee not only welcomes but pays good money for a highly prescriptive package, yet still understands that there is ample scope for the entrepreneurial flair and effort by which he or she can succeed. And the franchisor takes care to adjust the package continuously in response to customer experience.

A Chauffeur's Mission

Barry Brown of The Independent Assessment & Research Centre came across an interesting example of the positive impact of empowerment during a tour of the United States. He was visiting American hospitals as part of a study of information systems for the UK's National Health Service. During a luncheon meeting with the president of the Henry Ford Hospital in Detroit Brown was given a detailed account of the hospital's mission. Later Brown was driven in a hospital limousine to the airport and he fell into conversation with the chauffeur, who to his surprise reiterated the mission statement Brown had just heard from the president almost word for word. The driver told Brown that the Henry Ford Hospital aimed to be the most highly-valued, most advanced total hospital and health system in Detroit. He said that about three times a year groups of hospital staff meet with a trainer to learn about the hospital's achievements and future plans; they are asked for their opinions, and any revisions of the hospital's mission statement are outlined. Asked what he thought of the idea, the chauffeur said it was the first time he felt he was in a job where he was doing something really useful.

The driver then quoted to Brown the story of the man sweeping the floor of a hangar as NASA, who was asked what he was doing by a visiting consultant and replied: 'I'm putting a man on the moon'.

Figure 4.1 Durcan's Control Box

Timing of Control	Corrective Action by the Individual (Internal)	Corrective Action by the Organisation (External)
Feedforward	Anticipating problems and taking personal initiatives Planning ahead for a vital sales drive, for example	Training manuals
Concurrent	Manager's 'Third Eye'	Supervision
Feedback	Reflection	Budgets

(*Source:* Jim Durcan, programme director of the leadership development programme at Ashridge Management College)

In Brown's view, the chauffeur's enlightened attitude stemmed from the fact that he was part of an organisation 'that was continually reviewing with its staff what they were all doing. The staff have got to value that. I expected the chauffeur to say it was a waste of time. He said exactly the opposite.'

But Rothwell of Henley Management College sees the potential for conflict between empowerment and other fashionable management techniques: 'If one's getting into the philosophy of what's happening, there are some contradictions, because quality management systems are about control and procedures and yet if you are really talking about empowering people and enabling them to serve the customer, people need to be free to think creatively and innovatively.'

Internal and External Controls

This is the dilemma for many organisations. How do you provide a sense of unity in an organisation and a clear focus on markets and customers while at the same time running an empowered, freewheeling organisation? The answer, according to a number of management thinkers, lies in corporate culture. It certainly seems to be what makes the difference with Japanese companies. Notes Durcan:

> *If you can use a corporate culture you can replace a lot of the corporate controls by internalised controls, if you like. You know what this company is trying to do; you know what it regards as acceptable standards of customer performance, those sort of things, so you do it automatically, but you don't have to do it from the organisation.*

Durcan has developed a controls grid (see Figure 4.1) to help clarify this aspect of empowerment. It basically distinguishes between controls that are imposed on the employee by the organisation (external) and controls that are self-imposed (internal). The internal controls come from personal drives, such as pride in one's work, self-esteem, a sense of responsibility. External controls relate to the boss giving strict instructions governed by disciplinary procedures and poor performance penalties. Durcan's grid also covers the nature of the controls themselves, breaking them down into *feedforward* controls, *concurrent* controls and *feedback* controls. Durcan elaborates:

Classically, organisations are very strong on external feedback controls. What's the most common device for controlling an organisation? The budget. How do you know when you've screwed this up? After the event. The organisation may then take some kind of sanction against you or admonish you, but it only works after the event and it is externally imposed by the organisation.

Accountants would argue that budgets are intended to be feedforward control mechanisms. This is what you have got, this is where you are going to spend it; keep on track and it is all OK. But the ultimate sanction is a feedback one.

In Durcan's model an external concurrent control is supervision, something most managers do a lot of. They walk around, they see what people are doing, they keep an eye on the job. If the subordinate is getting it wrong, the manager will intervene at the time and help to correct the problem. That is an externally imposed control through supervision.

External feedforward controls are traditionally things like training and manuals. Problems are anticipated, so people are trained before the event to avoid the problem occurring. Alternatively, you have a manual which says that in the event of this kind of failure with the system, this is what you do about it. Someone has thought about the problem in advance and the manual is there as a procedure to follow. Adds Durcan:

All of those are external controls; they all involve committing organisational resources to the identification of variations from the prescribed limits and then driving employees to do something about them. Feedforward controls are better than feedback controls because you fix the problem before it occurs rather than afterwards, in which case there is less of a blip. But it's still external, so you're tying up organisational resources to do it.

The alternative is you get people to do it for themselves, using internalised controls.

An internal feedback control, for example, could simply be the manager reflecting on his work over a period of time. He reflects on the way he has been doing his job and handling the people reporting to him and questions whether he could have done things differently or to better effect. If he decides to make changes in his operating style that is something he decides for himself. The organisation may never be aware of his decision to make changes. There is a strong learning element to this approach. The manager learns to do things differently through experience.

As far as concurrent internal controls are concerned, most managers have what might be called a 'third eye' with which they watch their own performance – am I handling this meeting well? Is the interview going well? Am I getting this point across? They are virtually supervising themselves as they go along. But the point is they are the judge of how they are performing and they make their own decision about taking simultaneous steps to amend what they are doing in order to produce better results.

The internal feedforward controls are the raft of things that managers do to avoid problems before they occur – preparing an important speech, planning ahead for a vital sales drive. Managers who employ feedforward internal controls don't simply wait for things to happen and stitch things together when they are faced with a crisis. They try to anticipate the problems they are likely to encounter, but they do it by using their own initiative rather than consulting manuals or rule books.

The more enlightened companies, that are aware of the importance of empowerment, are making efforts to shift from external to internal controls. It is not such a major switch as it might first appear. Most employees resist being regimented and behavioural science indicates that most employees want to do a job that fulfils them. MacGregor's Theory Y philsophy tells us that people quite like work on the whole; they are basically responsible and want to do a good job. It is the external controls that often hold them back from contributing as much as they would like to.

Employees often become so accustomed to operating under external controls that they lose any inclination to show personal initiative. When asked why they didn't make an adjustment to a piece of equipment that obviously isn't operating properly, they respond by saying it is not their job to make such interventions. 'I know that doesn't work, but you told me to do it this way,' or 'Of course the manual is wrong, but you've never asked me about it, so I've never changed it.' Observes Durcan:

> In a sense, what they are saying is that this organisation has never conceded my right to internal controls. You've never heard me when I've made suggestions; you've never asked me what I thought; you've only ever wanted to operate with external controls. Now you're complaining because I operate with external controls.

Durcan reckons that a good many companies realise the need to switch to empowerment and internal controls:

> I think many organisations understand in some kind of intuitive way it needs to be done. Given the increasing competitive pressures . . . waiting until there is a problem and then fixing it is very expensive compared to seeing the problem in advance and avoiding it, so the benefits of moving from feedback to feedforward are enormous.

Building an empowered organisation
Consultants Kinsley Lord argue that the way to build an empowered organisation is to start with immediate business issues. These might be to increase revenue, reduce costs, serve the customer better, raise market share, develop new products, or respond to new legislation, for example.

> Starting from real business issues – rather than from mission statements or from abstractions such as 'culture', 'participation' or 'better communications' – makes it easier for people to understand the purpose of change and their part in it. Experience changes attitudes, exhortation doesn't. The trick is to create informal teams at all levels of the

organisation, but particularly at the coalface, to find solutions. The experience of doing so helps people to learn to work together in different ways, enthused by the real improvements they can see and they have made happen. The management act of faith is to permit this, because it means losing some control and not being sure what the outcome will be, and because it generates an enormous thirst for knowledge and training.

Kinsley Lord emphasizes that changing the infrastructure of the company – its formal organisation, pay mechanisms, budgeting systems and the like – should come last, not first, in bringing about new ways of working. This is because doing so can only support, not actually generate, changes in attitude. Research in the US on success and failure in changing large companies confirms that the way to change hearts and minds is to help employees develop their own solutions to immediate business problems, and only then put in organisational changes to reinforce them.

Why does Britain lag?
If empowerment really does bring the benefits ascribed to it, why has it not taken hold in Britain to the extent that it has in the United States, Germany and Japan? Kinsley Lord offers three principal explanations:

1. The short-term outlook of British management, driven by historically high interest rates, a stop-go economy and little political common ground on what the business environment should be. This tends to inhibit sustained investment in changing the way an organisation behaves.
2. Failure to recognise that tight management – good financial control, minimum overheads, few organisational layers – is just the ticket to the game. It is not the same as enabling management which provides the release of energy and innovation in the empowered organisation.
3. Manager's view of the workforce as a cost rather than an asset. At best this means little mutual trust between employer and

employee. At worst, it means employers whose attitude to their own people is a mixture of fear and contempt.

The London consultants argue that:

> *The problem of building an empowered organisation is that it cannot be done by the methods of the command organisation. There is no continuous evolution towards it: it requires somewhere along the line an act of faith on the part of management. It is a profound challenge to those who have built thier careers by rising through the ranks of the command organistion.*

THREE FALLACIES OF THE COMMAND ORGANISATION

1. *The quick fix fallacy.* 'It takes sustained effort, years and millions of pounds to build a new plant, install new information systems and develop, launch and generate profits from a new product. But changing the way the whole place works can be done in a matter of months by the part-time attention of a few good people. And when you've done it, you're there – you'll have the organisation you want.'

2. *The single lever fallacy.* 'There is only one thing you have to get in place – it's called MbO or PBB or PRP or SLA or HRM (and when initials are out of fashion it's called employee involvement or organisation development or internal communications or cultural change). Then you'll have the organisation you want.'

3. *The top down fallacy.* 'What you have to do is think it all through at the top of the organisation and then cascade it down: new structures, new reward mechanisms or putting everyone through a training sheep-dip, or better still a whole bundle of things. Attitudes will change and then you'll have the organisation you want.'

(*Source*: Kinsley Lord Management Consultants)

From the Command Organisation	To the Empowered Organisation
Remote top management, concerned with strategic planning, management control, external relations	*Visible top management, providing a vision of the future which employees understand and share*
Middle management mainly about control, direction and downward communication	*Middle management mainly about inspiring and encouraging people and enabling change*
Individuals told what to do, with jobs defined as sets of tasks	*Teams 'contract' their contribution to the organisation, with jobs defined in terms of team role*
Status comes from job grade and place in the pecking order	*Status comes from contribution to the organisation*
Thinking is up and down the organisation, in functional 'drainpipes'	*Thinking is across the organisation, in cross-functional project groups and informal teams*
People stop learning	*People keep learning*
Energy is low	*Energy is high*

(*Source*: Kinsley Lord Management Consultants)

5. The Delegation Process

If a senior manager thinks purely in terms of parcelling out tasks, he will only delegate two kinds of work. Firstly, the chores that he finds least enjoyable and absorbing. Secondly, those aspects of his job that he cannot physically complete within the time-scale available.

This style of delegation has been dubbed the 'one man and his dog' approach. The subordinate is the dog, fetching and carrying, undertaking routine aspects of the work and providing general assistance. All the important parts of the task are retained in the hands of the manager.

Delegation should not be about allocating mundane tasks to keep subordinates busy. As with all other aspects of management, the intention behind the delegation is of crucial importance. In the view of Dr Barry Brown, a consultant psychologist with the Independent Assessment & Research Centre:

> Research suggests that delegation works – adds value to the management process – if in fact the motivation isn't to get work off your desk but to carry out the task in a more effective, more fulfilling way, in which goals are not just to get through a piece of work because the system says you have to, but because you're actually aiming to do something constructive, definite and predictable. You've decided what it is you want to do collectively.
>
> Typically you are talking about organisations which are aiming to add value in terms of quality of service to customers. But there are other things you might want to achieve which wouldn't be financially led. It might be safety, for instance.

Three Goals

There are three principal aims that can be achieved when delegation is carried out effectively:

1. *Getting the task done.* This, in most cases, is the main purpose of delegating a task. The manager is passing on a project that he would normally undertake himself to a subordinate he believes to be capable of performing the task as well as he might have done it himself. The manager gives authority to the subordinate to act on his behalf, although he still retains the accountability. To a lesser or greater extent, everyone in the organisation depends on the subordinate doing a good job.

2. *Developing the subordinate.* As we have seen in previous chapters, this aspect of delegation is now taking on prime importance. Empowerment has become the new credo and enormous efforts are being made to ensure that tasks are delegated that help a subordinate to grow in his or her job. This leads to a more motivated and committed workforce and unleashes latent talents.

3. *Providing an opportunity to assess the competence and commitment of subordinates.* Performance appraisals are held at infrequent intervals. Delegation should be happening day in and day out. It provides an ideal opportunity for managers to set subordinates tasks that stretch their abilities and put them under test. There is no better way to evaluate subordinates' skills and willingness to learn than by observing them as they perform valuable tasks that actually make the difference to an organisation's success.

There is a fourth aspect of delegation that is beginning to be adopted more widely – its potential as a means of performance coaching. This is looked at in some detail in Chapter 6.

Decide What to Delegate

Before starting the delegation process the senior manager first needs to reflect on his own duties and responsibilities. The Industrial

Society, which runs regular delegation courses, suggests that the delegator should review four key aspects of his or her own job:

- What do I do?
- Why do I do it?
- Should I keep it?
- To whom could it be delegated?

This requires taking a careful look at each of the tasks you carry out within the scope of your overall job and separating out those which you consider are essential for you to handle yourself and those which you can confidently delegate to others.

The most practical way of doing this is to make a list of all the activities for which you are currently responsible and classify them according to the following three criteria:

- Tasks you are compelled to retain and perform yourself
- Tasks that can be shared with subordinates
- Tasks that can be delegated in their entirety to subordinates

Analyse your current range of activities and take steps to eliminate any discrepancies in the way you *actually* delegate compared to the way you *ought* to delegate. Then you should examine the list of tasks you never delegate and question why this is the case. Is it because you have traditionally always held on to that part of your job? If so, maybe it is time to change tradition. Is it because you find it one of the most enjoyable aspects of your work? If so, maybe it is time to let someone else share in the enjoyment. Your decision should be governed not by what gives you the most satisfaction personally, but whether it is absolutely crucial for you to retain that particular task.

What Not to Delegate

The Industrial Society advises its course participants that there are four main areas a senior executive should definitely not delegate:

(a) Tasks beyond the skills and experience of the subordinate

(b) Confidential, security and policy matters restricted to your own level of seniority

(c) Matters essential to your overall control

(d) Disciplinary issues

It would of course be self-defeating to delegate tasks which none of your subordinates is equipped to handle. But be sure that this is the real reason why you are holding on to certain tasks. It may simply be an excuse for wanting to avoid the risks involved in passing tasks down the line. It may be that you do not feel anyone in your organisation is skilled enough to take on a particular task; but with training, someone might be able to rise to the challenge. The snag is you won't know unless you give it a try.

Check that you are fully conversant with the skills your subordinates possess. You may be assuming they are ill-equipped to handle a project because you have never seen them operate in that area. If you simply ask some of your subordinates how they occupy their free time you will probably be surprised at their personal achievements. You should ask yourself whether such achievements indicate that they could take on projects which you previously believed were beyond their capability.

There are, of course, issues which only you as the senior manager can handle. It would be imprudent, for example, to delegate decisions about salary reviews concerning your staff. This could give rise to serious conflicts of interest. You should be the sole arbiter of your staff's value to the organisation. Nor should you delegate corporate strategy issues, although there is nothing wrong with asking a subordinate to conduct some research that may help you to decide the future course of your organisation. Matters of security, policy and discipline will always be the senior manager's exclusive province. But this still leaves a multitude of projects that can be passed on.

Decide Who to Delegate to

Selecting the most appropriate person to carry out the delegated task is not as straightforward as it might seem (See Chapter 7). Technical competence might seem to be the main factor to consider, but it is sometimes a good idea to select someone from your staff who is not the expert on the subject matter. People mainly learn from experience and unless they are put to the test you will never know the full extent of their capabilities.

If you pass on a project to someone who is inexperienced in the area concerned, you will be helping to develop him or her as an individual and you will be broadening the expertise of your management team. It will also give you a good opportunity to see how flexible the selected person is and how good he or she is at acquiring additional knowledge. It will also help you to assess the person's promotional prospects.

Ascertain the Willingness of the Chosen cAndidate to Take on the Task

You may think you have picked the ideal person to delegate an important project to, but for one reason or another this individual may be lukewarm about the idea. This will often be the case if the candidate is not the obvious choice. You may have faith in the individual's ability to acquire new skills, but he or she may have self-doubts. It is important to make it clear why you have chosen this particular individual, and to emphasise that one of the objects of the exercise is to introduce the subordinate to new skills and broaden his or her experience.

It may be that the selected candidate is concerned that he or she will be encroaching on the territory of someone who is the acknowledged expert in this particular area. The delegator should reassure the candidate that this has been discussed with the expert concerned, who is perfectly willing to let someone else have a go.

There are, of course, many other reasons why the chosen candidate may be reluctant to take on a delegated project. He or she may already have a lot of work to cope with, for example, and feel that the extra duty would be too much of an added burden. The delegator should explore this. Can routine work be given lower priority? Is this the real reason – or is the chosen individual looking for excuses to avoid being put to the test?

There may also be personal reasons for the reluctance.

Personality clashes may be involved. The new task may oblige the chosen candidate to work closely with someone he or she is unable to get on with.

The delegator will have to judge how real these concerns are. If they seem exaggerated, every effort should be made to persuade the subordinate that the delegated task will help to further his or her career and that it is an opportunity not to be missed. If, however, it seems that the reluctance is based on well-founded concerns, it is probably best to look for somebody else. A task reluctantly undertaken is unlikely to be done well.

Check whether Additional Training, Resources or Authority are Necessary

If the project will take the subordinate into new territory, it is very important that these implications are thoroughly explored. Will he or she be able to pick up the necessary expertise while performing the task – or will it be necessary to undergo additional training? If the latter, where can the training be carried out and to what extent will it affect the time frame in which it is reasonable to expect the project to be completed?

What additional resources will the subordinate need outside the normal scope of his or her work? Will they be readily available or will the delegator need to invest authority in the subordinate to obtain them? What other authority will the subordinate need? Where will the resources come from?

Clearly, the subordinate will be severely handicapped if all these issues are not settled at the outset. If they are not, it is likely that the delegating senior manager will be constantly called upon to intervene when the subordinate runs into obstacles. This will be disruptive and undermine one of the main reasons for delegating in the first place – freeing up the time of the senior executive to concentrate on other pressing matters. It will also undermine the confidence of the subordinate and even perhaps torpedo his or her chances of success.

It is important to establish the degree of authority you are prepared to invest in the subordinate selected for the delegated project. The following guidelines can be helpful:

1. For each task to be shared or delegated, the degree of authority should be based on three approaches:

   - Proceed without approval
   - Proceed, but inform me of your actions
   - Obtain approval before proceeding

2. Inform the subordinate of the degree of authority you wish him or her to assume for each task.
3. Try to find assignments for which you can grant complete authority. It will save you time in the long run and give the subordinate a greater sense of satisfaction. Examine each delegated task to ensure you are not retaining too much authority.
4. Hold regular discussions with subordinates to determine whether you have given them the appropriate level of authority. Take note of their comments and concerns and take them into account when delegating tasks in future.

The delegator should leave as much control as possible in the hands of the people undertaking a delegated task, so that they have the satisfaction of completing the task under their own steam. That does not mean that the delegator takes no further interest until the project is completed or a crisis occurs. The delegator should monitor progress at regular intervals, and support and assistance should be offered whenever necessary. The delegator should be generous with praise when the subordinate appears to be doing a good job.

To some extent, roles should be reversed during the delegation process. The delegator should become a kind of consultant at the service of the subordinate, providing the necessary advice and support to ensure that the project is completed in the best possible way.

Taking Time to Explain

One of the most important aspects of delegation is clarity. If subordinates know exactly what is expected of them the risks of delegation are greatly reduced. Valuable time can be wasted if they receive inadequate or unclear instructions and guidance on delegated tasks. In the worst cases, subordinates produce results that bear little or no resemblance to the desired outcome, which is frustrating to all concerned.

The subordinate needs to know the boundaries of responsibility; when it is necessary to ask for the authority to make a decision; who should be involved in a decision. A more senior manager often knows instinctively when it would be a good idea to have a quiet word with colleagues before taking an important decision. A subordinate needs guidance because of lack of experience.

Monitoring Progress

It is important to monitor progress, particularly in untried areas of delegation. It is not enough simply to establish a final deadline; subordinates may not realise they are falling behind schedule until it is too late to complete the task by the final date. There are some simple guidelines to ensure that their progress is monitored in such a way that you are not breathing down their neck but which will save you from a last-minute crisis:

1. Ask subordinates to break their tasks into steps and to provide progress reports based on these discrete phases of the project. They should give a copy of the reports to you and keep one for themselves. This ensures that both sides are aware of how things are progressing. Depending on a subordinate's experience level, you may wish to become involved in the planning process to ensure that the progress reports are acceptable. This will also help to clarify mutual expectations regarding progress points within the assignment.
2. Working with your subordinates, establish dates for interim reports and keep a file of these reports.
3. Set aside time to work with subordinates who require personal attention.

A Guide to Delegation

Assessment Design Services, the Leamington Spa training agency, advises companies on how to delegate effectively. It has devised a nine-step guide on how to assign a delegated task that details the most important issues:

1. **Explain what has to be done and why the task is important**. Behavioural scientists have found that it is important for employees to perceive their work to be worthwhile and significant if they are to be motivated and satisfied. If they do not understand why they are asked to undertake a task or what importance that task has in the work of the organisation or department as a whole, it is difficult for them to feel that their contribution is of any great importance. Unimportant work is inherently unsatisfying.

2. **Delegate in terms of results**. Delegate responsibility for obtaining a particular set of results or a specific outcome. Whenever possible you should allow your subordinate some freedom to determine the means that will be used.

A military analogy demonstrates the rationale for this. Imagine a general issuing orders to a company commander in battle: 'Conduct a night assault using three quarters of your company supported by 15 tanks; advance half a mile and seize the crest of the hill ahead; dig trenches; set up communications and wait for further orders'. No initiative has been allowed to the company commander.

Suppose when the commander reaches the brow of the hill, he sees the enemy in disarray and realises that by advancing some two miles further he can cut off an important supply line. Under the orders he has been given, the best he can do is report back to the general and ask for further instructions. By the time the new orders reach him, the enemy will probably have had time to rc-group, making it impossible for him to seize the supply lines.

Alternatively, imagine a general issuing an order to a company commander along these lines: 'We need you to secure the left flank of our advance. I am concerned that the enemy will seize the hill overlooking our positions and use it to bombard us and prevent us from moving forward. You have available your company plus 15 tanks. I am relying on you to protect the left flank of the army.'

The company commander still makes a night assault, still seizes the hill. But now, seeing an opportunity to cut off the enemy supply lines and thus prevent re-grouping and further attack, he does not need to hesitate. He understands the objective and can take whatever action is necessary to meet that goal.

3. **Try to give the subordinate the entire task or problem – not a series of unrelated steps**. Another important psychological aspect of job satisfaction is the belief that we are personally responsible for the outcome of our efforts. Success that is down to us is much more satisfying than success that comes from other people's efforts. A group of employees charged with producing a total product have been found to be much more highly motivated than people working on an assembly line where their responsibility only involves some minor part of the overall process. In terms of learning, being given the whole task allows us to understand how the various stages fit together and why they are important.

4. **Encourage the subordinate to show personal initiative**. One of the devices skilled delegators use is to leave some part of the task undefined. The person doing the task is encouraged to use initiative to deal with that part of the overall problem. In terms of learning and motivation the difference is enormous.

5. **Delegate authority along with the task**. You should always make it clear to your subordinates what authority they have and how far it extends. It is equally important that you give them sufficient authority to complete the task without further reference to you, save in exceptional circumstances.

6. **Agree on a timescale or deadline**. When you delegate a task, you should always set a timescale. Make sure, by consultation, that the timescale is not unreasonable in the context of the rest of your subordinate's work.

We all have plenty of experience of the problem that is continually put off until tomorrow. Because there is no urgency or deadline, something else will always seem more important. Eventually the problem either goes away – which shows that it was unnecessary to deal with – or it suddenly becomes acute and we are thrown into panic.

Sufficient time is needed if the task is to be a learning experience. Reflection and maybe one or two false starts will be needed as well as the time needed to complete the task. Setting the proper deadline is important for motivation. Being asked to do the impossible is rarely motivating. It provides a reason to fail without feeling guilty. Forget the myths about great charismatic leaders of the past who continually demanded the impossible from subordinates and regularly got it. Most of those stories have been heavily embroidered.

7. **Check understanding before the person begins the task**. However well we think we have communicated, it is always wise to double-check a subordinate's understanding before they start. People sometimes get the wrong end of the stick through over enthusiasm. They may hear one part of the message and disregard another. Time spent in checking and clarifying saves later problems.

8. **Build in feedback and controls**. Do not delegate a task and then forget about it until it is due for completion, if you are delegating with the intention of helping your subordinate to learn a skill or gain experience. You need to keep an eye on what is happening and be ready to offer advice or help in a timely way.

It would be a poor driving instructor who took someone on their first lesson, explained what to do, then got out of the car and sent them down a busy high street on their own! Part of the process of providing reassurance to the person you are coaching is the knowledge that you are keeping a discreet eye on their activities and can step in before any disastrous mistakes occur.

Agree on times when the employee can tell you how they are getting on and steps or measures along the way which they can use to check on progress. Leave the initiative for reporting back in the hands of the subordinate. Don't carry out unscheduled checks. Help them monitor their own progress.

9. **Get off the field of play**. The coach must not be on the field with the players. You have to let them win or lose on their own. One of the most annoying habits that managers have is to delegate an important task and then, with increasing signs of nervousness, gradually take it back again. It makes the subordinate feel worthless and devalued. It defeats the whole object of the delegation. You must let go. The next stage that requires your involvement is the stage of reflection where you both go over the results, giving praise for what was well done, identifying opportunities for improvement and reinforcing lessons learned.

Problem Areas

Most problems with delegation can be attributed to managerial failure. Adrian Savage of Assessment Design Services maintains that three failings more than any other contribute to ineffective performance:

(a) *Lack of direction*. The manager delegates the task but does not make it clear what the task is about, what the objectives are, how it should be carried out, what the limits of authority might be or what the timescales are. The subordinate flounders along until in exasperation, the manager steps in and completes the job.

(b) *Lack of feedback*. Subordinates undertake a task and complete it, but never learn whether their actions were good, bad or indifferent. After a while this saps the strongest motivation. Some pointers on positive feedback are outlined in Chapter 8.

(c) *Inability to let go*. The manager never delegates anything of importance, despite fine words. Subordinates quickly learn that their role is to follow orders, fetch and carry and provide respectful applause. The manager comes to feel that it is impossible to attract any staff who show initiative, reinforcing the belief that 'if you want something done properly, do it yourself.'

Savage believes that delegation skills are greatly misunderstood:

Delegation is wrongly treated as an inter-personal skill in the same way that communication is an inter-personal skill – that somehow you can get people who are skilled delegators like you can get skilled communicators. I think that's wrong. I think delegation is primarily a matter of control, not communication. You can get people who are very poor at inter-personal skills, but are very good delegators because they are prepared to take the risk; they are prepared to give up a certain degree of control.

In Savage's view delegation, unlike inter-personal skills, lends itself to a structured approach:

'What you are really trying to do is ask: what's the outcome you want? Are you doing this in order to get a job done? Or are you doing it in order to get a job done AND develop the subordinate?'

If approached in this structured way, it is possible to come up with tasks that are not going to put the organisation at great risk. Tasks can be identified that are not going to make a major impact, but which the subordinate may well enjoy doing, providing it is made clear what his or her limits of responsibility are. 'To you, the manager, that might be pretty mundane and dreary work. To the subordinate, who probably hasn't done it before – or not done it very often – it's actually quite interesting and exciting. A minor decision from your point of view might be quite important from the subordinate's point of view,' ponders Savage.

Delegating in a Crisis

Some aspects of a job are easier to delegate than others. When Sir John Egan took over the controls of Jaguar, he found a distinct absence of delegation because the company was fighting for its survival. Delegation is rarely practised in an unforeseen crisis situation. Subsequently, delegation became virtually an article of faith at Jaguar. In *Shaping the Corporate Future* by Kevin Barham and Clive Rassam, Sir John (who is now chief executive of BAA, the airports, retailing and property group) is quoted as saying about his arrival at Jaguar:

> *It was a very authoritarian system because of lack of time. It was: do as you're told. But now we are developing, training managers and delegating responsibility down the organisation. We are trying to develop very high levels of delegation; some Jaguar managers have very high capital expenditure authority by contrast with other firms.*

However, Jim Durcan of Ashridge Management College takes issue with the idea that a crisis is an inappropriate time to delegate. In crisis situations, he argues, strategic issues can be paramount, because if the wrong strategy is adopted it can be fatal:

> *If that's the point when the strategic executive is going to be really hands-on, it sounds to me like there's some kind of a paradox. it is more difficult to delegate in a crisis, but you could argue that in a crisis, particularly when time is short, the communication taken up by trying to take all the decisions at the centre and then pass them down the line effectively is actually much more time-consuming than it is if you can delegate significant areas to people who know what they're about.*
>
> *If you arrive in the middle of a crisis that might be more difficult to do. If you've actually developed your people reasonably, when a crisis occurs you are going to be in a much better position to delegate to them.*
>
> *I think it has more to do with managers being reluctant to give up control . . . very often when time is short and the pressures are hard, the tendency for managers to adopt a kind of telling style rather than some sort of involving, participative or, ultimately, a delegating style is very strong. After all, if you become the MD you clearly must know best and it is only right and proper you should take the decisions.*

Delegating in Advance of Emergencies

There is an argument that the actions to be taken in a crisis situation have been delegated in advance in the best run organisations. This is the view taken by Alex Bruce, a Texaco field manager responsible for the Tartan offshore oil platform 100 miles north of Aberdeen.

Bruce controls his responsibilities, which include two other offshore installations, from his office in Aberdeen, so he has little choice but to delegate day-to-day operations to his offshore installation managers. It is physically impossible for him to oversee personally what is going on. But the action to be taken if an emergency arises has been well rehearsed and everybody knows precisely what is expected of them. Explains Bruce:

We are set up for an emergency. We practise for it offshore every week. So that if an emergency arises everybody does what they have to do. For instance, some of the electricians and mechanical fitters, led by one of the foremen, will take over responsibility for fighting fires. The chef becomes the first-aid man. You could argue they have been delegated that responsibility in advance.

At the same time, when a fire or some other emergency breaks out on an oil platform, there is no time to debate how to tackle it. Someone has to direct the emergency operations:

The time-scale is so immediate there's usually no time for feedback. Maybe you ask people if they understand what is expected of them, but apart from that you don't have any of the classical long conversations you have in delegation to ensure somebody understands the ins and outs of it. That has all been worked out in advance.

Similarly in matters of safety, Texaco staff are under strict instructions not to take personal initiatives outside the scope of their job description. If, for example, the crane operator involved in lifting supplies off a supply boat on to an oil rig is temporarily indisposed, it is clearly understood that it is strictly against company regulations for someone who is not specifically trained to operate cranes to take over.

Matters of safety are obviously areas where delegation needs to be strictly controlled, but in other areas where the risks amount to little more than the possibility of upsetting one's superiors, Texaco is rather more relaxed in its approach. Says Bruce: 'We have a slogan in this company that it is easier to ask forgiveness than permission!'

Bruce finds it infinitely more difficult to delegate bureaucratic and administrative responsibilities than the more prescribed duties involved in dealing with emergencies and offshore operations. Offshore field managers tend naturally to think in terms of narrow time horizons, dealing with routine operational issues. When it comes to longer-term issues, such as planning, they feel less comfortable. When occasionally Bruce has asked an offshore installation manager to take over his job in his absence, there have been difficulties. The stand-in has found the office work contrary to his nature and has had to seek a lot of outside advice. Adds Bruce:

'Generally, I have a number of people whom I can totally delegate my job to, although they tend to just keep the fires stoked; they don't usually embark on anything new while I'm away.'

Financial and Technical Decisions

Many managers feel a lot happier about delegating technical decisions than financial ones. The reason is not difficult to understand in Durcan's view:

> Could it be because so many UK managers are actually poorly equipped technically compared to the number of accountants we have around in managements in UK firms and what they are actually saying is: 'I will delegate those things in which I am not particularly competent; those things in which I am more competent I will hold on to'?
>
> That seems to me to be treating delegation as a topic where you are saying, 'what's in this for me?' when I would argue the criteria ought to be: What's good for the organisation and what's good for the people working for me?

Savage of Assessment Design Services suggests that technical decisions are easier to delegate because there is usually a yardstick to measure them by. A chief engineer, for example, can pass on decisions to a junior manager, who is also an engineer, because they are both trained in the same disciplines and know what the technical limitations are. 'The chief engineer has a yardstick for deciding whether he can trust the junior manager,' says Savage. 'But if you are a general manager and you are allowing a product manager in a sales department to take some important decisions, how do you decide that person is competent unless you know them? You haven't got an external yardstick.'

Delegating Legal Work

Legal companies are not noted for being in the forefront of management training, but increased competition is compelling a number of the UK's leading law firms to re-appraise the role of their partners. There is a growing feeling that law firms need to be more aggressive in their marketing and that partners need to broaden the scope of their management responsibilities.

London-based Speechly Bircham has introduced a training programme for its staff developed by a Canadian consultancy group called The Edge. The programme, known as 'Rainmaking', is a 12-module training package, one of which focuses on delegation. It is run in-house by Fiona McLaren, Speechly Bircham's personnel director.

Solicitors generally tend to resist the idea of delegation. One reason is that their work is very time-dependent. 'Solicitors are generally very conscious of their use of time for this tends to govern their bill to the client', says McLaren. 'They usually have their own time-recording targets to achieve and are personally accountable if they do not reach them.'

But she argues that making the best use of time is 'about more than self-management; it's about the return on the investment of managing other people; it is about priorities in terms of tasks and people's skills and abilities to achieve them.'

McLaren also notes that solicitors generally do not consider themselves leaders – another reason why delegation does not come naturally to them. She would challenge this general assumption, however: 'More and more there is an awareness that this must be the case: solicitors do have to achieve tasks, build and work with teams and they are responsible for the continuing education of junior solicitors, at the very least.'

McLaren has drawn up a list of the key steps solicitors need to take to delegate many aspects of their work:

1. *Apprise your assistant of the background.* It might be useful to have the assistant look over the file in advance. Reviewing the file together gives you the opportunity to explain the matter and its place in the overall picture. It is important to express any specific views you may hold, the priority and the likely result.

   Example: 'We already act for this client in a number of tax and employment matters. You will see from reading the file that we have here the makings of a fairly contentious contractual dispute. Some time ago they entered into a joint venture with another company on a government project, but now the relationship has soured.'

2. *Define your responsibilities to the client and outline the client's expectations.* Let the assistant know what the client expects in terms of reporting back and completion deadline. Having these firmly in mind will reduce the possibility of any surprises later on and will help keep the assistant on the right track.

   Example: 'Our client is concerned over the loss of revenue to his company because of this dispute. I told him that we would look over the agreements and other documents this week, initiate a statement of claim within two weeks and push for a speedy trial. If you feel at any time we will not be able to meet this deadline, I need to know immediately.'

3. *Communicate any limits to available resources.* Giving clear guidance on the matter's priority and quoted cost to the client will help ensure that the assistant meets the client's deadlines and also incurs no additional costs which may have to be written off.

   Example: 'I have worked on the basis that this will cost £X and that this will be your highest priority over the next two weeks.'

4. *Get feedback from the assistant.* Ensure the assistant's complete understanding of instructions by asking him to summarise the key details or steps. You may find this easier if you approach it

from the point of view of checking that *you* have communicated clearly.

Example: 'Can I check that I've been quite clear? Let's review the situation . . . Now, if you need to discuss it further, you know I'm available.'

This will reduce the likelihood of any potential misunderstandings later. It will also help the assistant over any reticence in asking for further clarification.

5. *Discuss your assistant's ideas.* By discussing your assistant's thoughts on the matter, you will reassure yourself that he or she has a good grasp of the matter and that important issues will not be overlooked. Contributing ideas is more motivating than merely carrying out instructions and will produce greater commitment to the success of the project.

   Ensure the assistant knows where and when to get help, should the need arise.

   Example: 'Have you any thoughts on how you are going to proceed?

6. *Establish a procedure to monitor progress.* Tell the assistant the extent to which you wish to be informed on progress. This will reassure the assistant that you are not abdicating responsibility and you will not lose your control.

   Example: 'Let's compare notes after your initial meeting with the client and we'll fix a time next week to got through your draft statement.'

McLaren sums up the advantages of effective delegation as follows: 'The senior lawyer's time is freed up for other responsibilities; the junior lawyer's skills are developed; and the client gets high quality work at the right price.'

David Masters, a litigation partner at Speechly Bircham, learned some useful tips about delegating on the Rainmaking course:

You might think it's terribly important to you and the client to get something done by the end of the week, but if you don't explain why it is important then the person you delegate to might have their own list of priorities and it might go to the bottom of the tray.

The course also set Nick Ivey, a partner in the property department of the law firm, thinking:

There have been times when I have probably given someone a file, told them who the client is, and told them to get on with it, and then wondered why they sat in a room for a few days and didn't progress it – or why they went about it in the wrong way.

Tips on Delegation

- Identify tasks you are unlikely to complete on your own and delegate a portion or all of them.
- Ask people in similar positions to your own the kind of tasks they typically delegate.
- Identify responsibilities you are personally handling that could be handled by one or more of your subordinates and delegate accordingly.
- Find ways to individualise delegation to meet the needs and abilities of your subordinates.
- When delegating assignments verbally, ask subordinates to summarise the expected results to ensure proper understanding.
- Seek feedback from your subordinates about whether the instructions you provide when delegating are too detailed, preventing individual initiatives.
- Arrange regular meetings with subordinates to ensure that delegated work is on track.
- Use delegation as a way of helping subordinates learn a function that is important for his or her promotion.
- Ask your secretary to help you track delegated assignments.
- Invite subordinates to set their own deadlines, but ensure they keep firmly to them. Only accept excuses when clearly justified.
- Don't allow a subordinate to dump a delegated task back in your lap for you to resolve.

- If a delegated assignment is not up to standard, get the subordinate to tackle it again. Never take it over yourself.
- Ask subordinates for ideas on how to improve your style of delegation and monitoring of results.

6. Performance Coaching

One of the consequences of the drive to de-layer organisations and make them leaner and more competitive is that there are simply fewer managers around to do the work. In recent years many large companies, like BT and BP, have eliminated huge swathes of middle managers. This has led to two adverse effects, according to Bernard Taylor, professor of business policy at Henley Management College. One is that there are fewer advisers around in companies to impart their experience and expertise:

> A lot of the work that used to be done by middle managers is now done by computers. So there is an attempt to remove layers of management, but in many cases we have cut out managers who made important contributions, like planners, marketing people, personnel people and training people. These were often very sage, experienced people, but instead of having them helping with their advice we've cut them all out.

The second impact of the de-layered organisation is that the managers left are so busy coping with the increased workload that they do not have the time to participate in training courses.

Henley Management College was the first such institution in Europe to introduce general management courses to prepare functional managers for leadership roles. The college reckoned that it took at least three months for a functional manager to learn all the skills demanded of a general manager. Professor Taylor regrets that today many companies are reluctant to release key managers for such long periods for in-depth training of this kind:

What used to be a three month course is down to a month course and the month is chopped into units of one week because they can't get away because their business has been reorganised, restructured, acquired, merged, disinvested or privatised or something like that. The speed of change is very rapid and these people are totally unprepared for it. I think there is a crisis developing both in the public and the private sector where we want to delegate to people, but we don't pay the money to train them.

Of course, planned career development can do this, but we are fooling ourselves in this country because money is not being spent on training – internally or externally. The evidence is that very few managers get away – I think the figure is two per cent – in any one year to be trained. This is not true of Germany, France and other Continental countries. It's certainly not true of Japan.

It takes a large amount of effort and time to train people to do these jobs. I don't necessarily mean going away on courses. It could be done in the evenings; it could be done by distance learning; it could be done by an in-company MBA programme. There are a variety of ways.

Given the reluctance – or perhaps inability – of managers to undergo lengthy training courses, the idea is growing that perhaps delegation can be employed in a way that partially fills the gap. There is growing recognition that delegation can be a useful on-the-job training tool that is effective all year round.

Delegating to Develop
Performance coaching is not the same as mentoring, which is normally carried out by someone remote from the subordinate's immediate working environment. The advantages of performance coaching, according to Adrian Savage of Assessment Design Services, are numerous. It requires no new resources (and therefore adds nothing to overheads); it doesn't cut across the normal chain of command; and it can be done every day, as opposed to conventional training courses which tend to be sporadic at best and the lessons learned soon forgotten.

The demand for coaching skills is growing as a number of

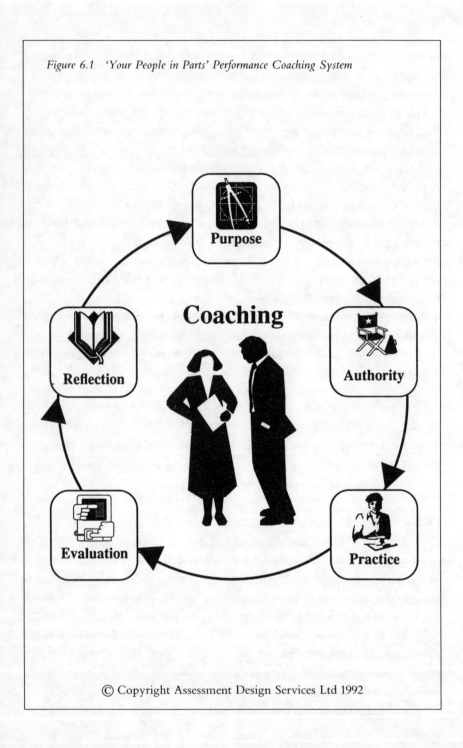

Figure 6.1 'Your People in Parts' Performance Coaching System

© Copyright Assessment Design Services Ltd 1992

innovative companies are restructuring to focus on the customer and turning their senior managers into coaches to support the front-line troops (see case studies in Chapters 10 & 11). This calls for a dramatic switch in style on the part of the senior managers, who no longer operate in a command and control mode, but provide support and counselling to those at the leading edge of their companies. At the same time, the front-line employees, often operating as self-managed work groups, find themselves empowered to take decisions that normally would have been the province of more experienced managers. Clearly, if the transition period is not handled with the utmost care, there could be serious implications for the companies undertaking these delicate experiments.

A PAPER Exercise?

Savage has helped a number of UK firms to introduce performance coaching. The system he has devised involves five stages which are encapsulated by the acronym PAPER – Purpose, Authority, Practice, Evaluation and Reflection (see Figure 6.1)

- **Purpose**. Performance coaching should always be undertaken with a specific *purpose* in mind. Perhaps the subordinate needs to learn a particular skill. Maybe he or she needs to gain particular experience or to improve standards in a specific area. Whatever the purpose, you must be clear about it. So must the person you are coaching. Nobody should be asked to undertake any development activities without knowing the purpose and objectives.

- **Authority**. To allow people to learn through their daily work, you must delegate full authority to complete the task. You must allow them to stand on their own feet. Delegate the necessary authority to take any essential decisions. Delegating tasks while keeping the important decisions in your own hands will not help people to learn effectively.

  Asking somebody to come up with a range of options from which you will make the final decision is sometimes effective, provided you can involve them in the decision or explain the outcome. This is not ideal. The best coaching situations demand that you let the subordinate have full responsibility and accept the possibility of a mistake. If you cannot allow a degree of risk, the task is not a suitable one for the purposes of coaching.

- **Practice**. People do not always get things right first time. If you expect instant results you are certain to be disappointed. The coaching process will quickly turn into a frustrating and acrimonious argument. You must allow people to face a situation a number of times, learning more each time they deal with it. Practice makes perfect.

- **Evaluation**. A coaching task differs from any other task because there is a conscious evaluation when it has been completed. To be a learning experience, you and your subordinate must take the time to consider the outcome and what can be learned from it.

  It is vital that you allow your subordinate to make this evaluation. We learn best from ourselves and our own actions. People learn very little from being given good advice by others. By thinking things through ourselves, we make evaluation real.

  Your role in this process is to provide feedback. This may involve giving your opinions, pointing out things your subordinate might not have considered, explaining possible repercussions and providing praise or constructive criticism.

- **Reflection**. People find it hard to recall large numbers of facts. It is much easier to recall a set of principles which can be applied to many situations. To derive general principles from specific actions demands reflection. We evaluate the outcome of an action, then reflect on it and discover what general principles can be abstracted and used for future guidance.

  Very few situations are identical to the ones in which the learning took place. If we can only apply our learning to identical situations, it will be of little use. Only by generalising a set of principles applicable to many situations have we gained a useful addition to our repertoire of skills.

  The manager or supervisor has a key role in helping

subordinates work through this process of reflection. You may need gently to encourage them to think about the situation by asing appropriate questions or by allowing them to explain their understanding to you.

Explaining to some other person what we think we have grasped frequently shows us gaps in our understanding. Teaching other people what we have learned is an excellent way of fixing it in our minds. Above all, you need to allow people time to reflect. Time spent in learning a lesson to last a lifetime is well worthwhile. Hurrying to the next task ensures that the same mistakes will be repeated.

Higher level decisions

Performance coaching is important when it comes to higher level decision-making. Savage points out that when delegation is simply a question of parcelling out mechanistic tasks, it is not difficult to do. But when it involves authority to take personal initiatives, it is a lot more difficult to control. Take the case of the receptionist, mentioned in the chapter on empowerment, who took it upon herself to deal with the overdue order before the manager responsible had returned from lunch. She was taking responsibility that involved her understanding of the company's procedures and her knowledge of what was generally expected in a situation of that kind. Without that knowledge, she could have made a bad situation worse. Maybe, the order was delayed because the customer had failed to pay an earlier bill or the consignment did not fulfil all the required specifications. Observes Savage: 'That's in an area where it is much more difficult to carve work up. If you're delegating a manual task it's very easy to split the job up. You know how long it takes to do X, Y or Z. Also, you have this problem of trust. How do you know if you can trust the person? It's much vaguer and yet it's much more important.'

Performance coaching is a way of exercising more control over the vaguer elements of delegation as well as developing the skills of the subordinate. Savage strives to get across three important aspects of performance coaching to the companies he advises:

One is to make clear that coaching is not about being nice to people. It's not about having a welfare officer type of role. Coaching is about getting the job done better by your subordinates. Secondly, I try to show them that delegation is in fact the principal tool of coaching, because it's no use sitting down and talking to someone like a Dutch uncle if you never then allow them to do anything. Most people learn by doing much more than by listening. Thirdly, I try to make it clear that there are an enormous range of times in which you can delegate but you, the manager, stay in control.

This is the bit that frightens people, because delegation is often presented as all or nothing – the empowerment literature is a good example. You're either a nasty autocratic dictatorial kind of manager who never allows anybody to do anything at all or you are one of those wonderful empowering, transformational leaders who doesn't appear to do anything except wander around in a sort of pink haze of charisma. Most managers are concerned about control because they are held accountable.

You've got to convince people that they can control it, so you start in a small way. You maybe start delegating on a reasonably consistent basis with people who you know and trust.

Intention

The difference between delegating simply to get the task done and delegating with the aim of developing your subordinate is all to do with intention. In the case of the former, the subordinate is set a task within a given time frame and either succeeds or fails to perform, in which case he or she will receive the approval or disapproval of the boss.

If you delegate in order to develop someone, on the other hand, you are using delegation as a coaching tool. You have to make the time available to sit down with the subordinate to talk about what has been learned from the exercise, whether it was done well or badly. A lot of managers will claim they don't have the time for such in-depth analysis. But a short-term sacrifice can lead to a long-term advantage. Once subordinates start to master the higher level responsibilities you steadily pass on to them, you will find your own work load reducing to the extent that you can concentrate on the strategic issues you are really there to solve. Once subordinates become skilled and you can trust them with higher level decisions, you can start to adopt more sophisticated techniques like management by exception.

The real advantage of performance coaching is that it is an on-going process that can be practised day in and day out, steadily building up confidence and expertise. Notes Savage:

A major problem I have as a trainer is that people are sent on a course and it becomes very obvious after a short time into the course that their principal concern is not that they don't like the course or they don't understand it or they are not getting anything out of it; but that when they get back to their organisations they are not going to be able to use what they have learned. Yet people are sent on courses almost knowing they're not going to be able to do anything when they go back. It's not only a tremendous waste of money – but also look at the effect on their own morale, their worth, their own feelings of self-esteem. Here I am learning something; when I go back I'm not going to be allowed to use it.

Differences between old style delegation and performance coaching:

Old Style Delegation	*Performance Coaching*
1. Delegate solely to get job done	Delegate to develop subordinate
2. Don't delegate decisions	Delegate decisions that don't have major impact initially. Gradually delegate more important decisions.
3. Don't take risks when delegating	Accept there is always an element of risk when delegating.
4. Admonish subordinate when he gets it wrong	Accept mistakes are inevitable. Use them as a learning process.
5. Don't waste time discussing results of a delegated task	Take the time to reflect on outcome of delegated task with the subordinate.

7. Delegating to the Right Person

I was once asked to write an article addressing the question of whether management is a profession in its own right. In other words, could a solid, professional manager take over at the top of any industry and be equally successful? I put the question to a range of corporate leaders and opinions were divided almost equally down the middle. Some argued that management was indeed a profession in its own right and that a top manager worth his salt could run any industry regardless of his background. There was no reason why a senior executive who had spent years running a retail group could not be just as successful applying his leadership skills to a car manufacturing company. It was not the job of top managers, they suggested, to be fully conversant with all the technical aspects of the operations they are running. They simply gather around them a group of expert colleagues they can call on whenever necessary to advise on operational details.

Other senior executives argued just as vehemently that if a top manager understands nothing about car engines he will inevitably fall flat on his face trying to run an auto factory. The debate will probably never be resolved. But there is no argument about the fact that a senior executive's chief responsibilities are to concentrate on strategic issues and represent the company to the outside world. Even if he is an expert in every aspect of the company he is running, he will not have the time to get involved in all the minutiae. He needs to have around him a team of managers he can trust and who can explain just enough about a technical problem for the top man to be able to make a sensible decision.

A Question of Trust

When selecting the best candidate for a delegated task, technical competence is obviously one of the first considerations. But most top executives will tell you that another vital factor is trust in the person taking on the responsibility. Lord Tombs, the former chairman of Rolls-Royce, the aero-engines group – he retired in September 1992 – puts it this way: 'You can't just delegate uniformly. Delegation is highly variable, I find. You can trust one guy totally, another 80 per cent, another one only 20 per cent.'

Lord Tombs learned to delegate the hard way. Early in his career he was working for the electricity supply industry as an operations engineer at a power station. The power station operated around the clock and Tombs was responsible for both day and night shifts. But of course he could not be available twenty-four hours a day, so he had to master the art of delegation. If there were any problems while he was off duty, he would be informed about them by telephone and he had to make up his mind whether it was something he should attend to personally or delegate to somebody else:

> It was quite character forming in the sense that you had to judge at some distance away whether the guy was capable of coping with the situation or not. It was a very useful period in my career, because you came up against people with confidence in themselves and people who were scared of themselves.

Sir Graham Wilkins, the former chairman of Thorn EMI, takes the argument a stage further. He maintains that a top executive should pick people who are capable of taking on devolved responsibility when he selects his management team:

> An important aspect of management that I have been aware of from an early stage is that you have to be able to choose good people and that's not an ability everybody has. You have to be absolutely certain that once you've picked somebody you actually give him the responsibility and make certain he undertakes that responsibility. You help him in all sorts of ways – you send him on training courses, advise him and educate him – but you must be able to delegate.

The obvious way to find out who you can safely entrust with delegated responsibility is to adopt a process of trial and error, but this can have its complications, as Adrian Savage of Assessment Design Services points out: 'It's a bit like saying: "I'm going to find out who's a good brain surgeon. I'll get a whole group of people off the street and let them do an operation and see which one manages to get the patient through it". It's the sort of risk nobody wants to take.'

Delegation by Degrees

Tony Knight of Henley Management College suggests that a policy of delegation by degrees can help to avoid disasters when a senior executive is unsure of the capabilities of his immediate subordinates:

> There are those things which you can fully delegate to somebody else and rely on them to get on and do it; there are those things which need to be done in a collaborative way, where your expertise and guidance is needed, where you need to maintain control because you're developing someone and you want to keep an eye on what they're doing. That requires regular report-back. Then there are those tasks that can only be partially delegated, where you want someone, if you like, to run around and do things for you, but it's your job. There are different levels of delegation.

Savage suggests that delegating managers should draw up a hierarchy of decisions to reduce the risks. Some decisions are so important the manager will decide to keep them for himself; other decisions he might allow to be taken by subordinates he trusts and there are probably a whole range of decisions he is prepared to take much more of a risk on because they do not put the organisation in much jeopardy.

When delegating to a junior manager for the first time, the prudent executive begins with the responsibilities that are at the base of the hierarchy of decisions. 'You're not going to let your subordinates bet the company on their decisions, but there are lots of things that don't really have too much impact. OK, if it goes wrong maybe it's embarrassing, but it's not a great problem,' maintains Savage.

Situational Leadership Model

American management experts Paul Hersey and Kenneth H. Blanchard have developed a 'situational leadership' model that attempts to match management style with the 'maturity' of the subordinate. They define maturity not as age or emotional stability, but as a desire for achievement, willingness to accept responsibility combined with competence and experience in relation to the complexity of the task.

The US experts believe that the relationship between manager and subordinates moves through four phases – a kind of life cycle – as subordinates develop and 'mature' and that managers need to vary their leadership style with each phase.

In the initial phase, when subordinates first enter the organisation, a *directing* mode of leadership is most appropriate. Subordinates have to be instructed in their tasks and familiarised with the organisation's rules and procedures. At this stage, a non-directive manager causes anxiety and confusion among new employees. However, a participatory employee relationship approach would be unsuitable at this stage because subordinates cannot yet be regarded as colleagues.

As subordinates begin to learn their tasks, a directing style of leadership remains necessary, because they are not yet willing or able to accept full responsibility. However, the manager's trust in and support of subordinates can increase as the manager becomes familiar with them and wishes to encourage further efforts on their part. At this stage the American experts advocate a *coaching* style of leadership.

In the third phase, subordinates' ability, motivation and desire for achievement have increased and they actively seek greater responsibility. The manager no longer needs to be directive. At this stage the manager should adopt a *supportive* leadership style. As subordinates gradually become more confident, self-directing, and experienced, the manager can reduce the amount of support and

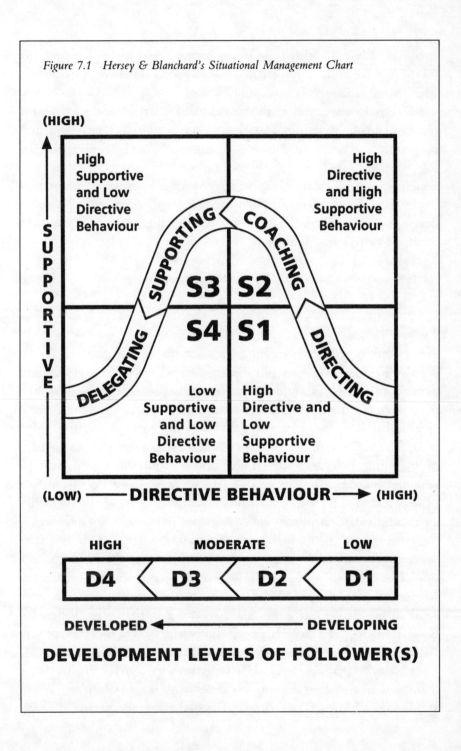

Figure 7.1   Hersey & Blanchard's Situational Management Chart

encouragement. By this time subordinates are ready to act on their own initiative and no longer need or expect a directive relationship with their manager.

The main attraction of the situational leadership model is that it recommends a dynamic and flexible approach to managing and delegating. The motivation, competence and experience of subordinates must constantly be assessed in order to determine which style combination is most appropriate. Hersey and Blanchard argue that if the most suitable style is applied at each phase of development it will not only motivate subordinates; it will also help them move towards maturity.

Figure 7.1 illustrates how management styles should vary in relation to the maturity of the subordinate undertaking a delegated task.

League Table

Some experts advocate drawing up a league table of the people the delegator has available to him, listing their characteristics, skills and experience. These should be matched against the nature of the project to be delegated. Is it a task that demands considerable technical skill in a particular area that only one individual can supply? If so, the choice is obvious. If, on the other hand, it is a project where only a modest amount of technical skill is required, which could be supplied by a number of people, the answer could be to create a project team to tackle it. The project team could, however, be led by a person the delegator is trying to develop, but who is not necessarily the person with the highest level of skill in this area. 'You've got to see the resources below you not in strict hierarchical terms, but as a pool from which you can draw a team', says Knight of Henley Management College. 'A lot of the organisations who are now sending people on our courses are working in that way. When the boss wants to get a project going, he or she draws together people from different disciplines to create a team.'

Henley Management College structures its courses to encourage team work and the sharing of skills and responsibilities. When syndicates are formed to tackle a particular issue, the person chairing the meeting is normally someone who has little expertise in the subject. It is emphasised that the chairperson is responsible for everybody else in the syndicate acquiring the necessary expertise – a much broader role than simply chairing the group discussions. For most managers it is their first experience of taking charge of a project that involves one of their weakest skills. Sheila Rothwell of Henley Management College says 'We make the point that if you are going to be any good as you go up the organisation you've got to be able to rely on experts and trust people and not always be one of those people who want to do everything yourself.'

In the commercial world, there is an element of risk involved in seeking to stretch your subordinates by putting them in charge of projects in areas where their expertise is weak. Rothwell points out, however, that most areas of innovation involve risk:

A lot depends on the motivation of the individual concerned. It is often possible to acquire a lot of expertise very quickly if somebody is motivated to do so. It is possible to take a crash course in the information required if you're motivated. Quite often, by doing that, you start asking questions which are just the sorts of things you should be asking, whereas if you had been in the sector for ten years you wouldn't.

Rothwell recalls that one of the best syndicate leaders she has encountered at Henley Management College was a schoolteacher who had joined a general management course. He particularly wanted to learn about marketing: he had no marketing experience, but he was appointed the syndicate leader for a complex marketing simulation exercise. In Rothwell's estimation, the schoolteacher was one of the best subject leaders she has ever come across: 'He certainly worked at it, but he didn't try to do it all. His skills were actually allocating the roles in the group, getting people co-ordinated, getting the decisions punched in every half hour and getting the discussion and the learning processes out of it.'

Avoiding the Obvious
Picking the obvious candidate for a delegated task is not always the answer. The managing director of a training organisation supervised

a team of ten senior advisers who ran courses. When a new member was recruited to the team, it was the managing director's responsibility to familiarise the newcomer with the fundamentals of the job. However, he decided to delegate the responsibility to one of his established advisers. The idea worked well. The senior adviser responded well to the prospect of taking on a new challenge. Recalls the MD:

> *Everyone benefited. The senior adviser felt quite pleased to be entrusted with a new responsibility. The newcomer benefited because the senior adviser was able to spend a lot more time with the individual than I would have been able to. The department benefited and I certainly did because at the end of six months I had somebody who could do the job reasonably well.*

When some time later another person was recruited to the team, the managing director decided to repeat the exercise. He delegated the responsibility again to the senior adviser who had done so well previously, but this time it did not work well at all, probably because the senior adviser found little challenge in tackling the exact same assignment all over again. The managing director should have given the responsibility to someone else on the team – even perhaps the previous newcomer.

Delegating to the Wrong Person

Managers are often tempted to delegate to prove a point. Maybe they feel threatened by a high-performing subordinate and they want to demonstrate that life isn't easy at the top. They delegate a task they feel pretty certain the subordinate will fall down on. There are two dangers attached to this. If the senior manager succeeds in his underhand ploy, the subordinate's confidence will be shattered. He may become a little more humble, but it will do nothing for his morale and may easily undermine his future performance.

If on the other hand, the subordinate succeeds in performing the difficult task with flying colours his ego will become even more inflated and his manner even more unbearable.

Sometimes executives delegate out of annoyance. I once became very irritated when a member of the editorial team I headed constantly complained that the quarterly planning meetings I organised were nothing more than a talking shop and achieved precious little. His complaints became so persistent that I thought up an idea I believed would put him in his place.

I decided to delegate to him complete responsibility for the next planning session. If I had adopted this approach because I genuinely believed it would develop this particular individual my decision would have been commendable. But I had ulterior motives. I knew from long experience that quarterly planning meetings took a lot of organising. Writers who are working hard to meet publication deadlines have to be persuaded to set aside time to study particular topics of interest and to prepare speeches which they know their colleagues are not particularly keen to hear.

The complaining member of my staff was probably the worst person in the world to delegate this task to. He had a lot of assets, but organisation was not one of them. His desk was always littered with paper and he could never find his notes when there was a query on his work. When he travelled he could be guaranteed to lose his passport or get on the wrong plane. However, I had one goal in mind. To get him off my back and to silence his long-standing criticisms.

Needless to say, the planning session he organised was a complete shambles. He had not briefed the participants properly; they were confused at receiving instructions from someone not noted for his clarity of thought. By mid-morning the meeting was in disarray and it was quite obvious it was not going to achieve any of its aims. I sat in the corner gloating over his discomfort, but my triumph was short-lived.

My immediate boss had decided to sit in on the session and was dismayed to find so little being achieved. In the coffee break he called me to one side and demanded to know why I had delegated such an important occasion to someone who was palpably not up to the task. I explained what my intention had been, but this did nothing to allay my boss's acute disapproval. He pointed out that even if I had proved my point, it was at too high a cost. Nineteen other members of the editorial team would spend a wasted day just so I could sort out a difference I had with one of my staff. Even more importantly, the planning session delivered nothing in the way of new ideas for future editions of the magazine. The whole exercise had been abortive.

What was even more frustrating was that the complaining member of staff did not even admit that he had made a mess of the planning session and continued his criticisms unabated. To achieve nothing positive in my relationship with this man, I had wasted a lot of good people's time and cast serious doubt in my boss's mind about my own abilities to manage. There are some lessons you learn the hard way. I never after that used delegation as a means to silence critics.

Characteristics of the High Performer

There has been a certain amount of research into the characteristics of a high performer, but Savage argues that intelligence is still the best measure:

> One of the things that has been ignored in favour of the soft end of behavioural science is the aspect of intelligence. All the data is – and has been for years – that the best single predictor of superior performance in any field is intelligence. Intelligent people in general are better at whatever they do than people who aren't. But because this was seen, particularly in the 1960s and 1970s as being elitist, an awful lot of work was done on behavioural aspects and personality traits.

Most organisations, in Savage's experience, place a huge premium on persuasive extroverts. But he argues that if you actually look at the way people use their minds you have a much better way of predicting who you can delegate to with confidence.

> It's not just raw brain power, like the horse power of a car. It's also how they use their mind. People are more or less fully formed by their early twenties; they don't seem to develop much after that in terms of intelligence. You might get a lot more experienced, a lot more

knowledgeable, but you don't change much in intelligence. Intelligence seems to determine what aspects of something you tackle and what you think is important.

Research carried out in the US into executive intelligence – or what Savage prefers to call *nous* – is throwing some new light on the issue. Some UK multinational firms have also looked into the mental attributes along with the personality traits, that are crucial for predicting who is going to be able to handle the kind of decisions required at senior level. The research shows that some people in their early twenties, who may be lacking in experience and knowledge, actually have the mental capability to handle top level decisions. The view is emerging that the results are better if you delegate to an intelligent twenty-year-old than someone in his fifties who has lots of knowledge and skills, but lacks the *nous* to make high level decisions.

These findings are difficult to apply in the real commercial world, however, because they more or less conclude that some people are born with the ability to take on high level responsibility and others aren't. That runs counter to the egalitarian grain of much of today's management thinking. It certainly raises questions about empowerment which tends to assume that everyone performs more effectively if let off the leash.

However, a lot of the work that senior executives ought to delegate is not necessarily within the scope of high level decision-making. Ideally, when a senior executive knows his management team well, he ought to be able to delegate according to their strengths and weaknesses. But Savage questions the practicality of this:

In an ideal world everybody would be in the right sort of job and you could delegate different things to different people; they would all be seen as being of equal value and everybody would be happy, but we don't live in the ideal world. Often the range of things you can delegate is quite limited.

The other problem is that some abilities are more highly valued than others. Most organisations tend to value doers – the people who go out and get things done. They are much more highly regarded than researchers, for example – people who beaver away in back rooms – even if they do occasionally come up with revolutionary ideas. So if a senior manager identifies someone on his team who is a good researcher and delegates accordingly, he may not in the long run be doing a lot to further the person's career. On the other hand, if the manager delegates work outside the scope of the researcher's talents to try to stretch him, the results could be disastrous both for the individual and the organisation.

Playing Safe

Savage argues that the senior executive should pick the people who are going to get the job done rather than take a lot of risks with people who have no proven ability in the area to be delegated:

> If you have someone who is a lousy salesman and you discover by an extended process of testing and analysis that they've got an amazing talent for agriculture and you're selling paint, there's not a lot you can do about it. One of the things that has bedevilled the whole area of delegation and coaching is the sort of social do-gooder aspect that implies that in order to coach it means you have got to be a kind of social worker and you have to believe that everyone is full of wonderful talents and if they appear to be stupid they aren't really; it's just appearance and life has been unkind to them.
>
> I much prefer to say to managers that they will come across people who are stupid. Don't waste your time on them. But if you come across somebody who is intelligent, who is capable and keen to learn – don't treat them as though they are stupid. It's like any other investment decision – you make your major investment where you get your most return.

Beware the Whizz-kid

Nearly every organisation has one – the whizz-kid who outshines all his peers with his phenomenal work rate and his non-stop deluge of creative ideas. He is usually completely over-qualified for the job he currently occupies and straining at the leash for promotion. He would seem an ideal candidate for additional responsibilities and an obvious target for your determination to delegate. But the whizz-kid needs careful nurturing and is not quite the godsend he seems to the over-worked boss.

At first you will be elated at your good fortune and remarkable insight at having hired a young, thrusting, high-powered subordinate. But before long your self-congratulation may well give way to frustration, because a whizz-kid is potentially more harmful to your organisation than an employee who doesn't measure up.

A whizz-kid can destroy the carefully nurtured morale of your management team by constantly shattering work records and production standards. He will throw into confusion everyone who falls significantly below his staggering work rate and, however good he is, he will hardly compensate for the loss of effectiveness of all your other employees.

He might even threaten your position as boss. Most whizz-kids are no respectors of rank except in their own aspirations to climb as quickly as possible to the top of the ladder. They will certainly bombard you with more ideas than you can handle. The constant stream of innovative suggestions won't let up, even when you make it clear that you are under pressure working on a major project.

The whizz-kid will expect you to be instantly reactive and as agile of mind as he is himself. The dilemma for the employer is how to harness all this energy without allowing it to turn the rest of the organisation into chaos.

The whizz-kid has often had a meteoric rise, sweeping all obstacles before him. He will probably have little notion of all the frustrations and political factors that a senior executive has to grapple with or the problems posed by human relations and budget restrictions.

Handled shrewdly, however, he can undoubtedly be an asset. Every organisation depends on bright ideas for its survival. If you can find a way to sift the gold from all the wild suggestions he drops into your in-tray, you will probably discover some practical ideas that can make your organisation stand out from the crowd.

But your first consideration has to be how to ensure that he doesn't ride roughshod over the sensibilities of the rest of your management team, many of whom may have given you long and loyal service. You have to do this not only to protect morale, but to protect him as well. For your team may turn on him like a pack of wolves if they feel he is about to ruin the carefully built-up cohesion of your department.

Your best solution lies in offering him some outlet for his prodigious abilities.

Find a special project that will keep his head buried in piles of computer print-out. Explain that you have never before been able to assign someone of his calibre to the project. Stress that it requires painstaking effort and you do not anticipate results for several months – or even longer if you can make it sound plausible. This will have the effect of diverting him from too much involvement in day-to-day operations.

Be sure the project you give him is not something that one of your more senior, long-serving employees would have cherished. You could be making matters worse rather than better if you appear to be turning the whizz-kid into your blue-eyed boy.

Of course you won't have enough special projects to keep him indefinitely occupied. This will only be a short-term measure, but it will serve to slow down his initial impetus and give you some breathing space to decide what you are going to do with him for the rest of the time he serves under you.

There are numerous ways to keep the whizz-kid in check while at the same time directing his talents to the well-being of your organisation. But several key factors are worth keeping in mind at all times:

- *Give whizz-kids tasks that show tangible results.* Whizz-kids are invariably hungry for achievements that demonstrate to themselves and their colleagues that they are making a real contribution. Ask yours, for example, to come up with a strategy to reduce factory wastage by a definite amount in a precise period of time. Don't give him airy-fairy tasks that leave him without any sense of achievement when completed.

- *Give whizz-kids tangible rewards.* In many ways, whizz-kids are like spoiled children. Because they have often shown great aptitude from their earliest years, they will have been constantly praised and admired and they expect this to continue into their adult life. By being generous with your rewards, both financial and verbal, you will help the whizz-kid to feel he is fulfilling expectations that people have had of him since childhood.

- *Respond quickly to the whizz-kid's deluge of ideas.* Even if you have to be largely negative about the majority of his suggestions, get back as soon as you can to him on his ideas. Most whizz-kids are impetuous by nature and there is nothing worse for them than to be kept in doubt about whether you think enough of their ideas to give them serious consideration. It is better for them to get a rebuff than no reaction at all.

- *Encourage whizz-kids to take up external interests.* Whatever measures you take you are unlikely to absorb completely the burning ambitions of the true whizz-kid. So try to divert some of his energy to external pursuits. For example, if the chairman wants to set up a company-wide task force to review the corporate ethics and social responsibility aspects of your organisation, put your whizz-kid forward as a possible candidate.

You may come to the inescapable conclusion that the whizz-kid is under-utilised in your department in relation to his true potential. But you should be cautious about recommending him for promotion too soon. Whizz-kids are often intolerant of others who don't demonstrate the same degree of intellectual acumen as they enjoy. In senior management, technical ability is often less important than the skill of getting things done through other people.

Some whizz-kids suffer from incurable egotism and whatever you do to blunt the adverse impact they have on your subordinates will be ineffective. In such cases, there will be little alternative than to seek to transfer the whizz-kid to a job where he can wreak less havoc. But be careful first to exhaust every opportunity to harness him. Otherwise your request might look as though you see him as a threat to your own job.

This may indeed be the case. Whizz-kids are nothing if not ambitious. And you may be left in no doubt from the moment he joins your staff that his aim is to unseat you. In such a case, it is probably worth taking something of a risk. Give him some important task that you are pretty certain is beyond his experience and capability. Choose an assignment you know is fraught with complexity and political minefields and perhaps also runs counter to corporate ideals.

If he falls flat on his face, it will bring him up sharp and make him realise he is not quite as brilliant as he thought he was. He will be particularly grateful to you if you come to the rescue and bail him out of the mess he has got himself into.

There is the danger, of course, that if the whizz-kid really is exceptional he may accomplish the apparently impossible assignment with flying colours. Accept it gracefully and bask in the reflected glory. Your survival then becomes a matter of being associated with bringing out and developing his talents. You can justifiably put forward the whizz-kid – now as your protégé – for the next available promotion and step out of his way as he rockets past.

8. Feedback

Letting employees know how well they are performing is an important part of a senior executive's job at any time, but during the delegation process it takes on even greater significance. Feedback helps to decide whether delegation is being conducted effectively, both from the point of view of the manager and the subordinate.

- *Positive feedback spreads*. Not only does feedback reward high performers; it makes clear to everyone what constitutes a good performance. It also makes good work a desirable goal. The knowledge that a good performance is recognised and rewarded will also spread a sense of fairness among employees.
- *Negative feedback should be a last resort*. The more effectively and consistently good work is praised, the less need there will be to criticise poor work. In many cases, a lack of praise is the most effective way of communicating a need for improvement. The senior manager can then spend more time helping the subordinate to improve rather than having to detail where the mistakes were made.
- *Benchmarks are essential*. The way feedback is given and the form it takes determines how effective it will be in improving job performance. A simple congratulatory pat on the back for a job well done may offer a momentary lift, but it is not a real incentive to continue to perform well.

  It is more helpful to measure, where possible, what goals are expected to be met to achieve success. Positive feedback can then be based on reaching or exceeding these standards. Where results cannot be quantified, specific comment ought to accompany praise or criticism, explaining exactly why a piece of work is being judged excellent or poor.

- *Feedback should be immediate.* Feedback is a form of learning. The individual who receives it learns what mistakes were made and what achievements earned praise and are worth repeating. People learn best when an 'answer' immediately follows a 'question'. At work the question is: 'How does my boss think I am doing?' The sooner the answer is provided, the more quickly and clearly the subordinate will be able to act in accordance with it and learn from it.

  Such immediate feedback is not always practical, of course. No manager or supervisor can keep an eye on every subordinate all the time. Work standards can provide a kind of do-it-yourself evaluation for employees.

  At lower job levels this can involve setting specific quantities of tasks or output to be accomplished within a given time frame. For subordinate managers or professional employees, work standards can be goals that are set when an assignment is made or discussed. But occasional direct feedback from a superior is essential. It is the way an employee knows that his or her efforts to meet the standards mean anything.

- *Varied feedback is more effective.* Even the most sincere smile of congratulation can become routine. Every manager should practise a variety of ways of letting people know how their performance is viewed. It can be done formally and occasionally at performance appraisal sessions; frequently and publicly during routine tours of inspection; and informally and privately as matters arise. It can even be done indirectly. A word of praise dropped to other people will invariably get back, magnified, to the good performer concerned.

Too often job performance and job satisfaction are regarded as separate issues. It is only when feedback enters the picture that the proper relationship between the two becomes apparent. People have an innate need to work and achieve. When their performance is properly recognised, that need becomes satisfied.

Giving praise for work well done does not come easily to many British managers, in Adrian Savage's experience, however:

British managers in particular give praise as though it involves the loss of a limb. I once ran a course in which I forced managers to praise one another and you've never seen a more miserable looking group of people in your life! But if somebody praises you for something, you have a natural tendency to repeat it to get praise again. We all like praise.

Similarly, if someone criticises you for something, there is a natural tendency to avoid it next time. So at the evaluation stage of delegation managers need to find everything possible to praise. They may have to criticise, but if that's all they do the subordinate won't be very motivated. The skills of feedback are vital in delegation.

Linda Chick, head of personnel at Cow & Gate, the Wiltshire baby foods and clinical nutrition company, agrees that praise is given begrudgingly by too many managers. 'People grossly undervalue the impact of praise. It costs absolutely nothing. There's not much in today's business environment that costs nothing. You can get enormous response from the odd "well done" and encouraging pat on the back.'

Cow & Gate has adopted an Open Style management approach which positively encourages feedback. Notes Chick:

In most companies there's a lot of feedback downwards but very little going back up the line. At lot of our Open Style is about challenge and questioning the obvious. Why am I filling in this form? Who is going to look at it? How is it going to improve my customer service at the end of the day?

Employees at Cow & Gate are learning that they need not feel bashful about pointing out areas where their managers may be impeding the effectiveness of the way they work. On the opposite side of the coin to praise, Chick believes that forgiveness is another important element:

If you do empower somebody and give them the freedom to go off and develop something and it goes wrong, don't beat them about the head with it. Examine what lessons can be learned to stop it happening again. Otherwise people will be living in fear of retribution.

Limiting Upward Delegation

Encouraging upward feedback is very commendable, but senior managers who hold on to too much control are in danger of becoming victims of an overdose of upward delegation. In a corporate climate where personal initiatives and risk-taking on the part of subordinates is positively discouraged, the senior manager is likely to become deluged with minor decisions. On the other hand, passing responsibility down the line and showing no further interest in the employee's progress amounts to abdication. It is not always easy, however, to strike the right balance between over-supervision and abdication.

Many senior executives have mixed feelings about what their subordinates should and should not bring to their attention. On the one hand, they need to be kept in touch with what is going on.. They do not want to be caught unawares by unexpected events about which they should have been informed from the beginning. On the other hand, senior executives lead busy lives and don't want to be bothered with decisions that can, and ought to be, dealt with at lower levels.

Because they have not yet resolved this problem in their own minds, some senior executives confuse their subordinates by contradictory reactions. On one occasion, the executive praises a manager for bringing a matter to his attention. But the very next time the same subordinate reports on a similar development, the executive snaps: 'Why are you bothering me with this? Surely you can take care of that?'

Such inconsistency is more inclined to reward the subordinate who is best at deciphering your moods than the one who correctly gauges the matters that ought to be put before you.

I remember when serving my national service in the Royal Army Pay Corps, I was put on duty at the guard-house with an empty rifle and fixed bayonet. For the two hours of my watch I had the awesome delegated responsibility of maintaining the security of the base. I suppose my authority was my rifle, although without any ammunition it was hardly a potent force. The sergeant-major, a vociferous man with a mercurial temperament in the time-honoured tradition of sergeant-majors, paid a visit to the guardroom and as I knew him well it did not occur to me to challenge him. He duly castigated me for letting him pass unhindered. He argued – somewhat irrationally I thought – that he could have been someone else in disguise. I took the lesson to heart.

The next time I was on guard duty and the sergeant-major approached I instantly went into the 'Who goes there?' routine and challenged him by thrusting my bayonet within an inch of his ample stomach. Again I was castigated. Surely, I could recognise my own sergeant-major when I saw him? It was the enemy I was supposed to challenge not my own side! There was no consistency in the sergeant-major's instructions, but you learned to accept such eccentricity in the army and you certainly never questioned the orders of non-commissioned officers who could make life very difficult for you.

There is obviously no precise formula for deciding what you as a senior executive should handle and what you should definitely delegate. Every executive adopts a style of leadership that best suits his or her temperament. But there are certain guidelines that should be observed if the senior executive is to avoid being burdened with minor issues that should not be their concern. Your subordinates should not trouble you in the following circumstances:

- *When the subordinate simply wants to cry on your shoulder.* Your subordinate should try to gain your respect, not your sympathy. You should not, for exmple, have to spend your time listening to a hard luck story about an order that was lost because of the arbitrary behaviour of a difficult customer. And you should not be asked to lend a sympathetic ear when an occasional rush job puts a subordinate under temporary pressure.
- *When a problem can more easily be solved by someone else.* You are undoubtedly the first to recognise that, just because you are the

boss, you do not necessarily know everything. Shrewd subordinates also recognise that seeking out expertise is a better course than seeking out status. You should therefore refer a subordinate without hesitation to someone who can readily provide the solution to a problem. The wise executive surrounds himself with experts who have knowledge at their fingertips so that he himself does not have to become bogged down in technical details. Your subordinates should learn that these experts are there to serve the organisation and that you are not the fountain of all wisdom.

- *When it is an internal problem arising within a division or department.* Managers are paid to control the internal workings of their groups and should not try to draw you into such areas. Thus, you should be informed about, but not consulted on, such matters as minor changes in office discipline and new departmental methods and procedures.

- *When a problem can be solved by subordinates themselves by applying more effort.* When your staff come to you to solve problems they themselves should be able to handle, it is a sign that they are not pulling their weight. Similarly, when your people come to you to get facts or figures that are readily available elsewhere, they are either being lazy or using the request as a pretext to see you on another matter they are finding it difficult to raise with you.

- *When the purpose of seeing you is simply to nag.* Even the most diligent executive occasionally needs reminding about an important deadline, for example. But when you have told a subordinate that you are working on something and you will get back to him or her when it is finished, the matter should not be brought up again. Or, if you have promised a decision by a certain date, you should not, prior to that date, be subjected to hints and demands for reassurance that you will indeed deliver on time.

- *When the purpose of the subordinate's approach to you is clearly self-protective.* Only weak, insecure managers approach their superiors to forewarn them that they are about to make a decision that will put them at risk. You should only be informed if the risk is of a major kind. If complications arise, subordinates should be discouraged from inundating you with evidence that they are not to blame, rather than tackling the issue themselves.

- *When the subordinate's request for a meeting is simply to pass on idle gossip.* In any dynamic organisation rumours and personal disputes will arise from time to time. That does not mean, however, that your managers should feel called upon to keep you apprised of such tittle-tattle. It is a waste of your time, and probably also indicates that the manager who comes to you with such trivia is under-worked.

Subordinates should, however, be encouraged to seek the senior executive's counsel in the following cases:

- *Where the implications could affect the organisation as a whole.* Managers have an ultimate responsibility to the organisation and one facet of that responsibility is to be sensors and relayers of potential benefits or threats to the firm. Subordinates should be encouraged, and not penalised, for bringing bad news immediately to your attention, just as they should be thanked for passing on good news. You should, for example, make clear to all your subordinates that you appreciate a warning about a potentially unsafe manufacturing process, or a suggestion to put right a faulty corporate policy.
- *When the ultimate resolution of a problem rests in your power alone.* You are the right person for a manager to turn to in matters requiring your authority or status. There are some letters your people may draft, for example, that need the added weight of your signature. And there are decisions and choices across a broad range of areas that only you, ultimately, can make final.
- *In the case of a decision that involves a diversion from, or change of, top management policy.* You are being properly consulted when, for example, an individual work group originates an idea that could affect an entire product line. Similarly, it is proper to consult you when a manger wants to become active in some political cause that might lead to a compromise situation for your organisation.

- *When the purpose of approaching you is to let you know an employee or a particular work group has achieved remarkable success.* One of your leadership functions is to recognise and encourage excellence. And, since you cannot be everywhere and see everything, your subordinate managers are acting properly when they bring to your attention examples of outstanding achievement, dedication or creativity. You should hear of individual triumphs, inter-group collaboration and record outputs, for example.

- *When the content of the information the subordinate wishes to impart would otherwise reach you from other, less sympathetic sources.* A manager is truly a colleague who warns you of a danger that he or she is not strictly obliged to tell you about. So you would count as valuable someone who warned you of dissension among the people immediately under you or of a rumour of an employee's unethical conduct. Being forewarned of such problems helps you to tackle them more effectively when they reach crisis point.

- *When the solution to a problem requires your unique talents and skills.* Aside from your formal power and authority, you will almost certainly have capabilities that are not to be found anywhere else in the organisation. It is certainly appropriate for your subordinates to call on them where they can further the major aims of your organisation. For example, because of your writing skills you might be the appropriate person to approve the official company history, even though it is actually somebody else's responsibility. Or perhaps your analytical ability would be invaluable in helping to cut through the undergrowth of a tough marketing problem, even though your status is not required.

The above guidelines will only influence the reality of the demands made on you if you draw the distinctions between what should and should not be brought to your attention by your subordinates. You can do that most effectively by your own consistent reaction to the matters they put before you. You should be appreciative of being informed of, or involved in, matters worthy of your attention. Deflect inappropriate matters by inattention or a simple statement such as: 'I don't think you need me for this.'

The obvious advantage of making clear the areas and limits of your availability is that your time will be more productively spent. The less obvious, but organisationally important, advantage is that, with you as a model, your subordinates will learn to allocate their time more wisely. The further down the management chain such discrimination seeps, the better managed your entire organisation will be.

While it is vital senior executives ensure they are not bombarded with petty detail, delegation is a two-way street. There will be serious problems if managers delegate to their subordinate and then take no further interest in the proceedings. Notes Tony Knight, director of the strategic management programme at Henley Management College:

Delegation is just one example of managing the immediate relationships at work. The immediate relationship downwards with the people who work for you is very important, but there is an equally important one which is upward. Managers have to learn to delegate things upwards. That is probably more difficult to manage than the relationship downwards.

It's a very uneasy sort of relationship and what tends to happen is that if you have something delegated to you, you go off and try to do it entirely on your own because it's the macho thing to do. You've been given this job to do, so let's get on with it, whereas what you really ought to be doing is seeing it as a mutual effort. It may be something that has been delegated to you to see if you can handle it or not, but that doesn't stop you from asking for help or guidance.

Knight argues that it is very important to keep the line of communication open with the superior during the delegation process, so that 'the boss understands what's going on and is sympathetic with what's being done and isn't likely suddenly to take an interest and step in and disrupt everything.'

Knight suggests that the senior executive who delegates a task should act as a kind of consultant to the person delegated to:

People need to feel that they can come to you for advice if they need it.

You don't want them to think they shouldn't consult you because if they do you will start getting involved in the detail. You want them to come to you because you've got a layer, if you like, above them of wisdom and practical experience that you can apply in a given situation.

9. Delegating in Founder-Managed Small Firms

Founder-managers of small businesses are rarely skilled at delegation. They have created their company with entrepreneurial flair and often at considerable risk to their personal finances. The product or service their company is selling was their idea and they have seen it through to success by negotiating a host of tricky hurdles. In such circumstances it is not easy to delegate important decisions to subordinates. Having survived numerous early crises, the last thing the founder-manager wants to do is put it all at risk by entrusting hard-won success to someone who might jeopardise everything.

Founder-managers are notorious for their autocratic, hands-on style. Stories abound of the lengths to which they go to keep total control of the company they have nurtured to maturity. But there comes a time when it is impossible for the small business entrepreneur to hang on to such omnipotent control. One morning he will wake up to find that he is no longer the custodian of a small business, but the chief executive of a medium-to-large company.

The transition poses problems that can be almost as threatening as the dangers encountered in the early stages of setting up the company. It is a natural instinct for entrepreneurs to try to stick with the management style that has successfully got them this far. It is easy for the entrepreneur to convince himself that nobody else, not even his closest and most loyal employees, can understand as he does what really makes the company tick.

But if he fails to relinquish his all-pervasive influence soon enough, he will lose control. It will become physically impossible for him to keep track of all the developments taking place. There will simply not be enough hours in the day. However, because the employees are accustomed to all the major decisions being channelled through the founder-manager, they will have grown up in a climate in which personal initiatives are not encouraged. It will take a clear signal from the company's owner to convince them that a new era has arrived.

Without such a signal, employees will feel stifled. Their ability to grow with the company will become stunted. Their personal potential will either never materialise or they will simply leave to join a company where their talents will perhaps be more fully appreciated and realised. In either case, it can be a serious loss to the original business at a time when it needs the support of all its employees.

A Different Style

The more far-sighted owner-managers see the dangers involved in hanging on to absolute power too long. It may take one or two minor crises to bring it home to them, but eventually they bow to the inevitable realisation that their company is in a different league and requires a different style of management. It is a time for autocracy to give way to professional management – for central control to be replaced by delegated responsibility.

This does not mean that the company has been badly managed up to this point. Indeed, if it was not being run efficiently it would probably never have survived as long as it has and some would argue that a good dose of autocratic management is appropriate for a small business in its fledgling stages. What has happened is that the company's operations have grown to such an extent that each department or division has become a mini-business in its own right and requires to be run as such by someone who has the authority to make decisions without having to refer back to the man at the helm all the time.

Once the founder-manager realises this, he has a crucial decision to make. Does he have the managerial talent within the company that he can rely on to share the load? Or must he go outside the company and hire 'professional' managers with a proven track record? Making the wrong decision can be calamitous. If he demonstrates a lack of faith in his own loyal employees by recruiting outside talent, he will of course demotivate them and lose their goodwill.

If, on the other hand, he is confident he has the necessary skills within the company's own ranks and that the only way to fulfil the potential of his own team is to put it to the test, he may be gambling on the future of the company. By the time he discovers that his faith was misplaced irreparable harm may have been done to a business it has taken him years to build up.

There are of course no pat answers to this dilemma. It is purely a matter of judgement. It is certainly true that some people never shine until they are plunged into the deep end. It is also likely that the founder-manager will find it very difficult to work alongside 'professionals' recruited from the outside who will be unfamiliar with his idiosyncratic management style. In that case, he will have little option but to fall back on the home-grown talent.

Making Garden Tractors

Just such a dilemma faced Gerry Hazlewood, who founded Westwood Engineering, the manufacturer of garden tractors. Hazlewood built the company from scratch. He began by bending pieces of metal in a garden shed to make simple rotary mowers. He built the original concept into a company producing tens of thousands of garden tractors a year and a turnover approaching £20 million. The company was so successful that it was eventually acquired by Ransomes, a much larger rival. But before that happened Hazlewood had to steer his brainchild through the phase of management maturity.

For some time he had been experiencing nagging doubts about the way the company was being run. One day it occurred to him in a blinding flash what the problem was. For a company of its size, then employing around 300 people, he was still playing too much of a hands-on role in management. Because he had built the company from scratch, he knew every inch of it and his influence was all-pervasive. Inevitably, he was cramping everybody else's style. In addition he was trying to handle more jobs than was physically possible.

As a result, some areas of the company were being neglected. In trying to grapple with the problems of rapid growth, for example, the company's quality control procedure had suffered. Recalled Hazlewood, looking back on that crucial stage of his company's development: 'I could see I was actually stopping the company from progressing.'

Believing that identifying the problem was three parts of the way towards solving it, Hazlewood decided no half-measures would do. He resolved to take more of a back seat in the running of the company. He handed over the managing directorship to his 32-year-old sales director and promoted his works and purchasing managers to the rank of director. He announced that in future the company would be run by this triumvirate of directors.

A Gift of Shares

Hazlewood remained as chairman, but to underline his resolve to withdraw from the day-to-day running of the company, he moved to a smaller office away from the centre of operations. Coinciding with this shift in managerial control, Hazlewood made a magnanimous gesture which left other industrialists aghast. He gave away a quarter of the company's shares to 35 of his most loyal employees.

Typically, Hazlewood made this decision on impulse. 'When I came to work in the morning, I had no intention of doing it. I had never thought about it before,' he recalled some time afterwards. But he did not believe it would have been sufficient to hand over management control without backing it up with a stake in the company. 'I don't think that would have been honest. That was the value I placed on them. They had supported me so fully. I had really been the administrator of their efforts,' he rationalised.

He dismissed any suggestion that he did it as a motivator: 'I have always refused to put carrots down for anybody. These people have always operated without carrots.' He did feel, however, that it would give them 'strength' to know that their decisions would now affect the value of their own shareholding.

It was typical of Hazlewood that he divided the shares among the longest-serving and most dedicated employees and not merely among the most senior members of his staff. Although the top three directors shared 20 per cent of the company between them, some of the beneficiaries of his largesse were working on the shopfloor. Hazlewood conceded that some more senior employees who had not been so long with the company might feel aggrieved by being left out in the cold, but he was in no doubt that he had rewarded the right people.

The new managing director took over determined to run things differently from Hazlewood's former quirky style. He set about delegating responsibility down the line and made it clear that middle managers would have a freer hand to operate according to their own ideas provided they met agreed business goals. He introduced departmental budgets for the first time in the company's history. Before, all the decisions on spending were channelled through Hazlewood, much to the consternation of the finance manager. Hazlewood would allocate the amounts to be spent on advertising, for example, according to his own gut feeling.

There was one responsibility Hazlewood did not relinquish, however, until his company was eventually sold off. Even after he had eschewed his hands-on style, he could still regularly be found mowing the grass outside the company's head office in Plymouth – with a Westwood tractor of course. There are some pleasant chores that entrepreneurs are simply not prepared to delegate.

10. Delegating to Teams

US management guru Warren Bennis, today an acknowledged authority on leadership, first came to pre-eminence in the 1960s with his prediction that bureacracy and hierarchical, centralised control systems would shrivel within the subsequent 25 to 50 years to be replaced by what he called an *adhocracy* of temporary project groups. Bennis then painted a picture of the fast-moving, information-rich, kinetic organisation of the future, filled with transient cells and extremely mobile individuals, which was highlighted in Alvin Toffler's seminal book, *Future Shock*.

Executives and managers in this system would function as co-ordinators between the various transient work teams. They would be skilled in understanding the jargon of different groups of specialists and they would communicate across groups, translating and interpreting the language of one into the language of another. People in this system, according to Bennis, would 'be differentiated not vertically, according to rank and role, but flexibly and functionally, according to skill and professional training'.

Because of the transient nature of the project teams, Bennis predicted there would be a concomitant reduction in group cohesiveness. 'People will have to learn and develop the loss of more enduring work and relationships.'

Bennis now admits that his vision of a world in which organisations are run by temporary task forces is taking longer to evolve than he had anticipated. But there is another evolution taking place that comes close to what Bennis foresaw. It is the tendency for organisations to do away with rigid hierarchial structures and replace them with permanent semi-autonomous teams grouped around a particular function or customer, for example. It is happening hand in hand with empowerment. Notes Sheila Rothwell of Henley Management College:

> *Empowerment in practice is often empowering teams as much as individuals. The group is made responsible for a section of the manufacturing process or a group of customers, so if a complaint comes in, that group is responsible for keeping that customer satisfied and making sure that everything connected with that order is dealt with.*

Rothwell makes the point that this is one of the distinctions between empowerment and the formerly fashionable concept of participation. Participation, she suggests, was a technique aimed at involving the individual more deeply in the goals of the organisation. Empowerment is a more collective approach and therefore attracts the notion that it is more advantageous to delegate to teams than to individuals.

This approach is not unlike the Volvo experiments in the 1970s where autonomous work groups were made responsible for the production of a complete car and for any after-sales problems that arose. The aim here was to win the commitment of the car worker by enriching his job and avoiding the monotonous repetitive operating style normally associated with assembly lines. The reasons behind introducing self-managed teams in today's modern company, however, usually have more to do with the need to push authority closer to the interface with the customer and the need to achieve greater productivity with slimmed down organisation structures. Rothwell notes that semi-autonomous work teams are being formed in a number of companies as part of the trend towards reducing the amount of middle managers in organisations:

> *A lot of team building is going on in organisations. If you take out lots of supervisors you make the team responsible for itself. There may be a team leader, but you give the team members training in group processes*

and leadership. Quite often, they deal directly with suppliers. This is a problem for middle managers. They realise they have lost power and control. Some middle managers are grabbing the power to themselves and making sure that not too much is pushed down the organisation.

But however much resistance middle managers try to put up, many management experts are convinced that self-directed teams are here to stay. One reason seems to be that senior executives feel much more confident about delegating to multi-skilled teams than to individuals. Stephen Taylor, chairman of management consultants Kinsley Lord, says:

The idea, which I think is a very powerful one, is that you are likely to be on better ground if you see the productive unit of the organisation not as an individual but as a team. Why? Because then the combination of the team can fill the peaks and troughs of an individual and because the strengths and weaknesses of different members of the team can compensate for each other. So a team is a stronger work entity than an individual. Therefore, rather than tasking individuals, you task a team to do something.

Taylor cites contrasting recruitment advertisements by American automobile companies as an indication of the new team-working trend. One advertisement asks for a spot welder and lists all the qualifications and experience the job requires. A contrasting advertisement for a spot welder emphasises that the successful applicant will be expected to be part of a team and lists the skills existing team members have and which the applicant will have to complement. 'It is a completely different psychology about what the job requires and the reward systems were different as well,' notes Taylor.

A lot of research into self-directing teams has been conducted in the US by Professor Quinn Mills of Harvard Business School. He has made a somewhat surprising discovery – that while the trend towards empowerment is persuading many US organisations to devolve power to semi-autonomous work teams, the teams themselves often adopt an autocratic style of management. The teams, in Quinn's experience, are rarely empowered themselves.

This throws an interesting light on developments at Sherwood Computer Services, a London-based software company that has dispensed with a hierarchical organisation structure and replaced it with 14 self-managed client teams. The original intention was that none of the teams would have a leader, but about half of them have in fact elected small executive groups to take control (see case study at the end of this chapter).

In the view of John Garnett, former director of The Industrial Society, delegating to groups that have no leaders will never work, simply because there is nobody to hold accountable. 'Everybody wants to be in on the decision. When it goes wrong nobody wants to know. You always have to delegate to a team leader. People who set up leaderless teams have never lived life. You cannot win a cricket match on a Saturday afternoon without a playing captain. Somebody has to be held accountable.'

Garnett maintains that any attempt to run teams without a leader is doomed to failure. There is nothing to be gained, in his view, by looking for alternatives to leaders by appointing facilitators, for example. In all the experiments in autonomous work groups in Sweden it transpired that the key person was the charge-hand, the person who gave the orders to the assembly line. Without such a person the operation fell apart.

Adds Garnett:

> It's the person who is in charge down at the place of work that is the key and that's eternal. If God had believed in committees he would have incarnated himself as a committee, not as Jesus. They used to talk about the ICI team. I don't remember a team with 150,000 players a side. They talked about the ICI family. I don't remember a family with 150,000 children. Those are not realities.

But the reality does seem to be that an increasing number of companies are attempting to replace old-style autocratic organisations with ones that devolve authority to self-managed teams which are given a high degree of autonomy within the constraints of a company's overall mission. There is still a great deal of experimentation going on and a lot of questions to be answered, but there is considerable evidence to suggest that those organisations prepared to try the teamworking approach are reaping a rich harvest of rewards in terms of higher productivity and a more motivated workforce.

Four different approaches to the idea of devolving responsibility to work groups – at Toshiba Consumer Products, Sherwood Computer Services, Rank Xerox (UK) Ltd and Digital Equipment Co – are outlined in detail below.

TOSHIBA CONSUMER PRODUCTS

Given that empowerment has its origins in the Far East, it is perhaps not surprising that one of the most interesting experiments in devolved responsibility to groups has been taking place at Toshiba Consumer Products, a Japanese subsidiary making television sets and air conditioners, based in Plymouth. Visiting the company's headquarters on the Ernesettle industrial estate is like stepping into a Japanese sanctuary. Above the reception desk a poster displaying the location of the parent company's factories all over the world proclaims typical oriental slogans – Idealism, Commitment, Enthusiasm. Two Japanese visitors are bowing low as they are greeted by a Toshiba employee in the blue jacket that is the company uniform worn by all levels of employees.

For over ten years TCP has striven to become a model of what harmonious industrial relations ought to be by combining the best of Japanese practices with the most cherished British industrial traditions. The slogans in the foyer are repeated everywhere. Talking to senior management you are told: 'We look for enthusiasm, idealism, attention to detail and commitment. We look for those before we look for expertise, because we can always train people in terms of expertise, but we can't train them in terms of attitude.'

The Plymouth experiment was born out of the collapse at the beginning of the 1980s of a Rank-Toshiba joint venture, which had lost its way. Only 300 of the former workforce of 2,500 were re-hired to form the nucleus of a new company. Devastating though that event was for the local economy, an opportunity was seized to start with a clean slate and to introduce concepts that could never have taken root in a company entrenched in traditional British industrial practices.

Toshiba was shrewd enough to realise, however, that it could not simply impose Japanese working ethics on a Western culture. On the other hand, perhaps it could take the most successful Japanese working methods and adapt them to the British scene, especially where they seemed an appropriate cure for some of the most endemic ills of UK industry.

It was decided to attack the 'them and us' syndrome by introducing the idea of single status. Everyone was employed under the same conditions. A 40-hour week, monthly pay and a combined restaurant for management and workers were essential ingredients of the egalitarian style. The nub of the Toshiba approach is a company advisory board (COAB), which meets monthly to thrash out any issue that threatens to undermine industrial harmony. Some 14 elected representatives from different sectors of the company sit on the board, which is chaired by George Williams, the managing director. Shopfloor representatives predominate. COAB can only advise senior management, but it is very rare for its recommendations to be ignored. It has become known as *negotiation by advice*.

In the event of a deadlock an independent arbitrator can be called in and both management and the AEEU, formerly the EETPU, the trade union, have agreed to abide by the arbitrator's decision. When the revolutionary approach was first announced to the world at large it was hailed as the first no-strike agreement in British industrial history and Toshiba became the focus of much attention in the management and general press.

The experiment soon delivered some handsome dividends. The Japanese parent company, clearly happy with the harmony achieved at Plymouth, later agreed to invest in a £3.5 million microwave oven factory at Plymouth, creating another 220 jobs, and a video recorder operation with a further 100 jobs. The parent group was reported to be considering Germany for the microwave oven factory, but its decision to opt for Plymouth was directly attributable to the successful experiment in new-style industrial relations. It led Des Thomson, TCP's managing director at the time, to declare: 'I won't say we've become a model industrial society; that's far too grand a way of putting it, but we've demonstrated that we can achieve Japanese standards of quality, good levels of productivity and we have a reputation for industrial harmony and for meeting business objectives.'

COAB has evolved in the way it operates. At the beginning, out of natural impetuosity to prove that it was not simply a paper tiger, its advice was often translated into action with undue haste, threatening to undermine the role of management, particularly the middle ranks. Then the pendulum swung in the opposite direction and there was an inordinate delay before recommendations were acted upon, so that all levels of the company could be consulted and give their approval.

Thomson eventually managed to strike a middle path. He aimed for Japanese style consensus and if he felt that the management representatives of COAB were happy with a particular suggestion, he wasted no time in implementing it. He was more cautious and followed strict formalities, however, when it involved a delicate issue, such as a decision to drop the traditional half-day holiday to mark the company's foundation in order to improve productivity.

According to George Harris, TCP's personnel director, the problem of middle managers feeling disenfranchised by the authority of COAB has been completely overcome:

> It is not a contentious issue any more. We keep management fully informed of what's going on at COAB. A briefing note is given to every manager along with COAB representatives immediately after the meetings. Managers are informed of key issues and any board level decision either is parallel with COAB or just ahead. So they don't feel undermined.

A series of training courses was also organised for shopfloor representatives of COAB to help them understand management problems better. As a result the level of debate at COAB has steadily risen. In the early days the meetings tended to be dominated by trivial issues concerning the lack of soap in the toilets or the need for some chairs so that people could sit outside in the sun during rest periods. Gradually the discussions turned to more weighty issues to do with efficiency and quality.

COAB was put to the test in 1988 when TCP had to announce redundancies, something it has always striven hard to avoid. As sales dried up the company battled hard to retain everyone for six months, but eventually had to bow to the consequences of a recessionary climate. Recalls George Harris:

> *That major issue was handled through COAB, not on a last in first out basis, but on a basis of who could we most afford to live without. We used appraisal documents to rate people. We looked at their disciplinary record – whether they were under any warnings or anything like that. All these factors were taken into account in deciding who should leave the company and it ended up being a cross-section of people of different lengths of service. It was done around the COAB table. The actual mechanism for deciding who would leave was agreed at the table and the appeals procedures – if anyone felt unfairly selected – all involved COAB. It was a high level of involvement in the business at a very difficult time.*

Similarly, COAB was involved at another difficult period when the Toshiba parent group introduced a European rationalisation programme and decided to source all its video recorders in Germany and Singapore and microwave ovens in France. This time there were no redundancies. All the people working in the Plymouth video recorder and microwave oven factories were redeployed either to the TV factory or to a new factory set up to make air conditioners. 'COAB made a big contribution to that whole debate,' notes Harris. 'As a management we clearly had to develop our own ideas and proposals, but we used COAB to comment on them and invited them to make other suggestions and change them, which they did quite often.'

Another issue hotly debated at COAB concerned how best to switch from a 40 hour to a 39 hour week. After much discussion, a novel solution was arrived at which saw the introduction of a system of three weeks of 40 hours and one week of 36 hours. That meant that everyone could look forward to a free half day each month.

Working schedules have since been modified to take account of the problem of seasonal fluctuations in demand. For the colour television plant, COAB came up with the idea that working times should vary in accordance with the amount of work available, thus avoiding the expense of having to hire some 30 temporary workers each year during the peak periods. They now operate a four and a half day week of thirty-seven and a quarter hours during the off-peak months of January to July and a five-day week of forty-two and a half hours from August to Christmas. The same base pay is paid all the year round with overtime where necessary. The new air conditioned factory will have its own variation to suit business needs.

COAB has clearly been the way forward for TCP, but Harris admits that the extent to which it can empower its workforce is limited:

> In the end, the process of making TVs is still very much to do with long assembly lines where people are acting as groups to achieve a result. So trying to act individually within that situation obviously has its limitations at the assembly line operator level. We certainly haven't got any flexible teams in the sense that they are constantly flexing. We have in the sense that people on the lines are very flexible as individuals and can work anywhere on the line and do anything. But I wouldn't like to say we are very far down the road to empowerment.

Toshiba in Plymouth recognises the practical limits to what it can achieve. COAB is working well and seems to meet its needs. There has been a decade of industrial harmony. Even though the power of the unions generally in British industry has waned, TCP's record is one of which it can justifiably be proud. The company embarked on a daring experiment long before the term empower-ment was generally recognised in this country and it has no intention of making any detours now.

The company's commitment to COAB is best summed up by Des Thomson, the former managing director:

> *I have a personal theory that when you embark on a progressive route such as this you should first of all recognise that you are moving up a slope. Unless you are continually innovative and thinking forwards you will go backwards. That's inevitable. I also firmly believe that if you embark on that sloping road, the road behind you falls into a large crater, which is then filled with fire and serpents, so there's no return route.*

SHERWOOD COMPUTER SERVICES

Devolution of authority, empowerment and performance coaching have become a way of life at Sherwood Computer Services, a London-based software company that has dispensed with a hierarchical organisation structure and replaced it with 14 self-managed client teams of between 25 and 30 people that report directly to the board. Each team is autonomous with its own resources and functional advisers. A central Business Team acts as a coaching and counselling resource, helping the client teams to develop broader skills and offering guidance when they seem to stray from the corporate mission or the agreed budgets and business plans.

Two main pressures prompted Sherwood to introduce such a revolutionary management structure: an urgent need to reduce costs and a determination to improve customer service.

The starting point was in 1988, when Sherwood lost £2 million and was close to insolvency. A major re-financing programme saved the company from collapse and there was an inevitable cost-cutting exercise that radically reduced the number of lower-paid employees. But Bob Thomas, who was then a non-executive director of Sherwood, was convinced that these measures were failing to tackle the root cause of the problem. He began discussing with his board colleagues the idea of introducing team-working as a way to improve client relations and slim down the organisation still further.

'There was an enormous need to improve our service to our clients and balanced teams – balanced in skill terms, having everything within them to serve the needs of a small group of clients – seemed a way of bringing that into being,' recalls Thomas, who subsequently became non-executive chairman of Sherwood.

His ideas at first fell on deaf ears, but persistence eventually won through. The trigger was a conference in London staged by Tom Peters, the popular American management expert. By coincidence Thomas and Richard Guy, Sherwood's chief executive, both found themselves at the same event. Thomas attended the conference as a representative of Ashridge Management College, where he has been a lecturer in strategic management for 18 years. Guy was there from Sherwood.

Peters was in good inspirational form and by the lunch-time break Guy had become as convinced as Thomas that self-led teams would provide the way forward for Sherwood.

Client Teams

The teams were formed around the clients that Sherwood had in January 1991 when the new structure was introduced. The company's three main customer groups are Lloyds of London, insurance companies and local authorities. The teams were designed to service fully one large client or a number of smaller clients in the same market sector. Each team has all the necessary skills to achieve that purpose – software development, servicing, maintenance, selling, administration. For example, the salesman's task within a team is to spearhead the acquisition of new customers and the sales of additional services to existing clients.

Initially, the central staff functions formed a separate team, but over an 18-month period these were gradually dispersed to the front-line client teams. Sherwood now has hardly any central services apart from the Business Team which provides the expertise for performance coaching. The accountants and book-keepers who used to provide a central service have been distributed among the client teams. Only the finance director and one assistant remain at the centre. The same has happened with the personnel and marketing functions.

Since there were not enough accountants to go round, some teams had to do without, but from time to time the accountants detach themselves from their various client teams and form what Sherwood calls a virtual team to tackle a particular project that might affect all the teams.

In the teams that were not allocated a central office accountant or book-keeper, the skills have had to be developed among team members who were not previously experienced in that area. 'That's a deliberate act,' explains Thomas. 'Our policy is to up-skill people to be able to get through more work with the same number of people. That effectively is what we are doing through multi-skilling.'

The teams operate almost entirely autonomously within agreed annual budgets and a three-year business plan negotiated with the top management board. The detailed annual budget is part of a three-year plan which is aligned to Sherwood's corporate mission.

'If they want to stray outside the budget, they have to come back to the board for more, but so long as they're on target nobody bothers them,' explains Thomas. 'If, despite coaching, a team goes off target, one of the coaches from the central Business Team goes in, like a pilot going on board ship, and takes over the team.'

Three Disciplines

On the few occasions that this becomes necessary, the intervening member of the Business Team may have to revert to a directive style of leadership until a particular problem is resolved. Such diversions from the straight and narrow are kept to a minimum by three levels of discipline, which, as Thomas puts it, 'keeps everyone pulling in the same direction.' The first discipline is the corporate mission.

That's quite extensive. It describes our chosen market and describes our chosen culture and style of operation of which team working is a part. It describes our size hopes for the future. The second level of discipline is the negotiation of those annual budgets, embedded within three year plans which are negotiated with the board. They are linked to the mission and the board ensures that they are.

The third level of discipline is a set of rules jointly developed between the team and the board, which is known as *the framework*. This lays down certain standards of performance, behaviour and quality, to which everyone is expected to conform.

A designated person in each team takes on a monitoring role to ensure that the disciplines are being observed. The board too keeps a weather eye on the teams. 'It is always talking to the teams in a counselling, helping, coaching role, so that the whole thing keeps fairly well on track,' explains Thomas.

Co-ordination across teams presents something of a problem, but even here top management keeps its distance. If, for example, three teams feel they would jointly benefit from the acquisition of a new mini-computer, they set up their own project team to explore the options and present their proposals to the board when an expenditure outside the agreed budget is required.

Although the client teams are free to operate as they see fit, they are expected to 'acquire the business they promised in their plan and to operate at a cost they promised in their plan, so that they deliver the correct bottom line and the agreed level of customer satisfaction,' as Thomas puts it.

Measuring Customer Satisfaction

Sherwood has a very structured way of measuring customer satisfaction. It undergoes what it calls 'a health check' every quarter by asking its clients to rate its performance according to criteria predetermined by the client. Team members' bonus earnings are partly determined by the degree of success in meeting the criteria, as judged by the customers themselves.

Sherwood sits down with its clients once a year to establish the key performance criteria. A list of approximately ten standards are drawn up on which Sherwood's employees are regularly rated.

Leaderless?

As might be expected with such a radical new approach, the self-managed client teams have not all had a smooth passage. The original idea was that none of the teams would have an overall leader, but since they were given the freedom to operate autonomously about half of them have in fact elected a small executive group. There is clearly a danger that Sherwood could have flattened its own pyramid only to create dozens of mini-hierarchies throughout the organisation, but Thomas is confident that this can be avoided.

He admits, however, that top management at Sherwood is not entirely happy with the idea of the client teams appointing an executive group.

We don't want it because we deeply believe that as soon as there is even a semi-permanent group like that the rest of the team can shuffle off responsibility and avoid the joint and several responsibilities we want placed on, and accepted by, the entire team. We prefer the view that there are several leadership roles to be performed within a team and that rarely can one person fill all those roles.

One leadership role that Thomas refers to is the need for someone to ensure that all the team's actions are in line with the company mission. That same person helps and guides the team through the development of its own mini-mission and is constantly ensuring that there is a strong linkage between the corporate mission and the team mini-mission.

Secondly, we see the need for a leader who helps the group develop its own goals and then works with individual members of the team to get personal goals established and contracted for, which will ensure the team as a whole delivers to its budgeted plans and promises. Then there needs to be someone who leads the social processes of the team. Yet another person is needed to lead the monitoring and evaluation of performance. All of those things are normally wrapped up in one individual manager. We don't think one individual can ever do all those things. Through education, talking and coaching, we are slowly working at encouraging those incipient hierarchies to go away. Whether they will or not, we don't know.

An encouraging sign for Thomas and the top management team

is that evidence is beginning to emerge that the truly self-managed teams that are without an incipient hierarchy are the best performers. 'The evidence is limited at the moment,' admits Thomas. 'I don't want to put it too strongly, but it is of course a tool for selling to the rest of the organisation the view that hierarchy doesn't produce the best results.'

Who is for Tennis?

It has not been an easy transition for senior management either. The coaching team itself is going through a learning process. Switching from a directive style of leadership to one of counselling takes time to master. There have been complaints from the client teams that there is still too much direction.

Sherwood has adopted a highly innovative approach to this problem. It invited sports coach Alan Fine of the Insideout Company, who is also a management consultant to companies like Dow and IBM in the US, to help train the coaching team. He initially worked with the Business Team members to improve their tennis skills. The lessons learned from the tennis coaching were then applied to their business role.

Halfway There

Thomas believes Sherwood is perhaps halfway towards the kind of organisation he and his colleagues set out to create. The feedback from the team members is encouraging. It indicates that the new approach of devolved responsibility is leading to more worthwhile jobs and more motivated individuals.

In his consulting capacity, Thomas advises Shell managers involved in a major change programme at the international oil company. As part of the programme, they are given access to Sherwood as a living example of an organisation undergoing a significant culture change. The Shell managers are invited to assess the progress Sherwood has made and make suggestions for carrying the process forward. That has given Sherwood the chance to obtain feedback from its staff via a neutral third party. Says Thomas:

> They always talk to quite a lot of junior people in Sherwood and from

that very open feedback there is no doubt that many people in the organisation now clearly recognise the opportunities for personal growth and for fully flexing their emotional, intellectual and physical muscles. I think it arises from the concept of joint and several responsibility. They know that around them there's a group of people who complement their weaknesses and allow them to use their strengths.

But there is even more tangible evidence that Sherwood appears to be following the right course. The £2m losses have been turned into a £2.4m profit – and not just as a result of cost-cutting. City analysts are predicting that the upward swing can be expected to continue. A doubling of Sherwood's share price is a further indication that sceptics in the City, initially unimpressed by the radical new organisation structure, have now been won over. In addition, there is hard evidence, because of the regular health checks, that the quality of Sherwood's performance as judged by its customers is steadily rising.

Inevitably, there has been a price to pay for such a fundamental change in company culture. Some people found the extent of the devolved responsibility and the lack of directive management too much to handle. At first they put up resistance to the changes and then, realising that the changes were going to happen anyway, many of them left the company. These were repercussions that Sherwood's Board had anticipated:

People with a high control orientation – and there are such – just go and we were prepared to accept the loss of even good people if they did not fit into the new organisation. We have stood those losses.

To some extent they helped fulfil one of the aims of the restructuring, which was to slim down the organisation. The number of people employed by Sherwood has dropped from a peak of 750 to around 360, but revenue per head has increased from around £35,000 in 1988 to £75,000 in 1991.

Loss of Status

Another cause of concern was loss of status, but Sherwood has partially solved this problem by imaginative compromise. The problem was compounded by the fact that the world at large has not yet come to terms with flat organisations. Customers like to deal with people in authority when they have issues to raise. Sherwood has therefore introduced conventional management titles for use in its interface with the outside world. The titles mean something to customers, but hold no significance inside the client teams. This serves a double purpose: it prevents Sherwood's clients becoming disoriented, and it also means that at a cocktail party, for example, a Sherwood team member can introduce himself as someone with a conventional title and avoid a lot of confusion.

A few team members have allowed the new-found authority invested in them under the system of devolution to go to their heads and have tried to grab more control than their competence justifies. Says Thomas:

> If you tell people they are autonomous they begin to take it seriously even if they are not adequately skilled. That is still happening today. That's why the coaches have to keep their eyes on people and why we have to explain to people that you can't be autonomous if you are stupid or ignorant. Since we still have some up-skilling to do, not all the work done by our coaching team is coaching; some of it is telling. In terms of Hersey & Blanchard's situational leadership, we still have to use telling and selling, not all coaching and consultation.

More Time for Strategy and Clients

The gains top management at Sherwood enjoy as a result of pushing responsibility further down the line are in accordance with all the classical theories of delegation. 'Time has been released to think more about strategy and to spend more time with clients, pulled in by the client teams,' says Thomas. 'It has also released time to concentrate on acquisitions, which we have declared as our main growth route.'

Digital Equipment Co.

Until the late 1980s Digital Equipment Corp., the world's third largest computer manufacturer, had enjoyed phenomenal success. It had been growing annually at a rate of between 30 and 50 per cent, supplying computers, software and computer services. It had built its reputation on outstanding technical know-how and the high quality of its products. The company had not needed to develop the same level of marketing expertise because its products were so well received in the market place they virtually sold themselves. It was also a good company to work for, according to Chris Lever, group effectiveness portfolio manager with Reading-based Digital Equipment Co., a subsidiary of the US parent group:

'There was a very strong founding culture, very clear values, a lot of entrepreneurial spirit. You could be what you wanted to be in the company – and genuinely so.'

Then came a serious setback. The projected business growth simply did not materialise. Partly through complacency, Digital's products had almost reached market saturation point. For the first time ever, it needed to take market share in order to grow – but it did not have a strong tradition of marketing acumen. 'We had some wonderful products, but we were still basically an engineering company and we weren't driving hard enough in the sales and marketing area,' explains Lever.

The setback showed up shortcomings in other areas. The company's cost structure had got out of hand and its profit margins plunged. The crisis caused Digital to review the way it was structured and how it was positioned in the market-place. The quality of its computer products was still its main asset, but it saw the service side of its operations, including consultancy, as the area with the most profit potential. It decided to market itself as a total solutions supplier, offering to advise companies on how to manage change, for example, when they installed new computer networks. Adds Lever:

'I guess we've undergone a heart-searching debate around what our product is. What do we stand for? What are we in business to do? What are we selling?'

Stripping Away

Hand in hand with this re-assessment of its market place, Digital has embarked on a substantial restructuring of its organisation. It has stripped out a swathe of middle managers, as part of a 20 per cent reduction in its UK workforce.

Salesmen become Entrepreneurs

At the same time a new operating style, aimed at achieving total quality and focusing on the interface with the customer, has been introduced. Explains Lever:

> *We realised that over the years, from being a very entrepreneurial company we had become a very bureaucratic organisation and that was actually hampering the way decisions were made and problems were solved. So we have taken a very clear step, which is to devolve as much of the decision making authority to the groups which are closest to the customer. For example, we have given our account teams as much authority as we possibly can. We now call them entrepreneurs because they are responsible for their own budgets and for how they spend and allocate their funds. They are also obviously accountable for the business they bring in.*

The senior managers who previously ran the sales teams are now known as coaches, whose prime responsibility is to offer guidance to the groups of entrepreneurs. Lever admits that not all the former senior managers have coped easily with the transition:

> *We've tried to get people to understand that calling them coaches is not enough. Unless they behave in that way they will still be an old-fashioned manager. That transition has been quite easy for some and difficult for others. We are supporting that with a training programme. Some of the former senior managers are going through that; others have had to pick it up as they go along.*

Digital has no intention of standardising its approach to self-managed work teams. It believes there will need to be a lot of experimentation and that different operating styles will emerge to suit a range of needs. Currently, it is experimenting with high performance work groups, based on a systemic way of working; championship teams; competency circles; and action learning groups. They are all moving the organisation in the same direction, which according to Lever, 'is about giving power to people, dispersing responsibility and accountability and promoting a very different way of working.'

High performance work groups, for example, are not dissimilar to the autonomous work groups pioneered at Volvo in Sweden. Instead of the work being divided up into discrete units, teams are involved with a product from conception through to final delivery and after-sales service. They are given total ownership of the process. Some pilot schemes in Digital are going well; others not so well. 'Where it hasn't worked so well, it is sometimes because the managers have not been supportive of the transition. It's a fundamental change,' observes Lever.

The Role of the Coach

Digital has always provided a great deal of freedom for its employees to go their own way. One of its value statements going back to its early years maintains that if employees are given responsibility and believe in the company they will do the right thing if left to their own devices. However, the new working methods Digital is pioneering have raised new questions about such issues as control, freedom of action, responsibility, authority and accountability. Digital has not always taken the same route as other companies experimenting in this area. For example, it believes there needs to be a manager – even if he or she is called a coach – to act as a mediator between the work groups and the rest of the organisation.

The exact amount of freedom of action each self-managed work team should have to operate effectively is still a matter of intense debate at Digital. Lever is responsible for advising on how the teams interlink within the organisation structure. According to him, there is a lot of 'in-depth discussion between the managers and the self-managed teams, not only to understand their roles, but what each needs from each other and whether the amount of authority that is actually being delegated is appropriate and is going to be helpful.'

Communication Channel

Digital's approach may change with time, but currently it believes that a manager, who might be responsible for as many as nine self-managed teams, is necessary to provide 'a communication channel' into the self-managed teams. Without such a channel, Digital is fearful that the self-managed teams might become freewheeling satellites that detach themselves from the main organisation and spin off in contradictory directions. But Lever insists: 'There is no standard model. There is no check list of these are the decisions you can take, these are the ones you can't.'

There are currently around 30 self-managed teams within Digital's UK organisation. One of them comes close to embracing an entire department. Others are in the sales organisation, finance, customer support, human resources and engineering. The issue of leadership within the self-managed teams is still evolving. Lever takes the view that leadership should be allowed to emerge. He counsels against self-managed teams appointing leaders at the outset. There is a clear danger of establishing mini-hierarchies that echo old-style command and control organisation structures.

> *We suggest that the teams very explicitly look at the issues of power and influence and recognise that you do need individuals who are more influential, who are more empowered, and for them to be an asset to the team and to be clear about their role. It will emerge from the teams rather than making appointments. It will be based on capability rather than on any historical precedent.*

Digital has only just embarked on an experiment that is taking it into unknown territory. But Lever is convinced that the fundamental shift the company is attempting to make is the only real way forward:

> *You can't get a truly problem-solving culture if you've got one*

person making all the decisions. You need to be able to release the authority to teams that feel part of the decision-making. All the evidence is that when you do that you actually get more effective, more productive teams and that shows up in the bottom line results.

RANK XEROX'S SELF-MANAGED WORK GROUPS

Rank Xerox (UK) Ltd has converted its entire customer service division into 250 self-managed work groups (SMWGs) of approximately ten employees each. From the outset the company determined self-managed work groups would become the natural way of doing business in its customer service division rather than something that was imposed on its managers. Explains Shaun Pantling, director of customer service: 'We didn't want to force it and we didn't want to have to continually reinforce it. We wanted people to work naturally that way, so we started off with that as the vision.'

The company also recognised that it would require a change in management style to facilitate the transition. It would basically mean a switch from directive management to advisory management, says Pantling.

We set ourselves a vision that says employees will set their own direction within a framework. Two of the key areas we saw in our vision is that members of the SMWGs would be self-appraising and they would be self-monitoring as groups with authority to control the distribution of such things as rewards and recognition. This would give employees a greater feeling of being part of their own company.

Teams are currently run by field supervisors, but the aim is to phase the supervisors out and replace them with team-appointed leaders who will probably operate on a rotational basis. 'They will elect their own leader who will be very much a strong facilitator and organiser and that's a role any of the group can play with training,' suggests Pantling. 'This is one of the hot questions around the whole work group philosophy at the moment – do you have a team leader or not? We think that you do, but we think he should come out of the team, rather than appointed by management.'

The teams are grouped by product, geography or customer. The group members, according to Pantling, 'come from similar backgrounds, similar educational levels and have similar objectives.' They are free to act autonomously within certain guidelines. These have been fairly explicit initially, but as the work groups gain in confidence and they grow in experience and skills, the guidelines will become less confining and allow an increasing degree of freedom of action.

For example, it used to be Pantling's job to decide whether employees in his division were allowed to work flexible hours. Now work groups are free to decide this themselves. One work group has decided to match its working hours with those of its major customers, achieving big productivity gains in the process. Similarly, the group supervisor used to decide at what stage an engineer needed to call for assistance when, for example, there was difficulty in locating a fault in a product. Now the engineers can take that decision themselves as well as deciding to whom they should take the problem. Adds Pantling:

We think the opportunity for empowerment is practically limitless. We are now looking at the idea of team appraisals instead of appraising individuals. We are also looking at ways the team could actually carve up their own salary increases. Instead of us doing it, they would apportion their salary increases. Already most of the teams are responsible for things like reward and recognition.

Adds managing director Vernon Zelmer: 'We have basically told the teams to run the business. You can't be half-pregnant – half-empowered. We say: "You're empowered, but within the work process. If it's within your work process, it's on your street, take licence. If you're taking a decision that is affecting another process, which may be the credit approval cycle, then you've got to do the interface".'

Rank Xerox has run into surprisingly few problems of incompatibility. Work group members seem to have adapted to the new style of operation with considerable ease. Les Jones, director of human resources, puts this down to the heavy investment in training the company has made:

If you don't do the training up front, you are likely to have problems. We are investing $1 million this year in just training self-managed work groups. You've got to train people. You can't just say: 'You're empowered; you're a self-managed work group; go away and get on with it'. You've got to train them and it's big bucks to put together the quality of training they need to be able to operate effectively.

In any organisation, however, there are those who will resist change of any kind and a small number of Rank Xerox employees have taken early retirement. Some who did not feel comfortable with the new operating style within the SMWGs have been redeployed. Pantling says: 'There are some people who will never go from the cynic–sceptic stage to the convert stage. They will always be sceptics or cynics and the organisation will flush them out.'

A layer of long-serving middle managers known as district after-sales managers were felt to be blocking the new approach and were taken out of the division to prevent a communications log-jam. Virtually all were redeployed.

Up to now work group members have not been given the authority to dismiss people, but Pantling believes it is only a matter of time. He is so convinced that the self-managed work groups are the answer that he has committed his division to 25 per cent productivity increases over the next three years and it is already ahead of schedule. 'We really do believe it will give us a significant payback in the area of productivity, materials management and probably customer satisfaction, because they are much closer to the customer. We think all areas of management will be significantly impacted by self-managed work groups.'

11. The Pace Setters

If empowerment is taken to its logical conclusion, delegation as it has traditionally been practised could well become extinct. Rank Xerox already believes that self-managed work groups have made delegation an obsolete term. Says Les Jones, its UK director of human resources: 'The responsibility and the authority is given straight to the team. When you take out the group of managers who had that responsibility suddenly the team has acquired the responsibility and the authority to do the job in one easy move.'

There are probably few – if any – companies as far down the road to empowerment as Rank Xerox. It is blazing a trail others are sure to follow. Other companies will find their own route and their own answers to the dilemma of how to devolve responsibility and authority while at the same time setting explicit guidelines that ensure everyone in an organisation is moving in the same direction and is geared to achieving the same corporate goals and vision. Without such a framework anarchy is virtually inevitable.

The case studies below illustrate the various ways companies are attempting to resolve the devolution issue. No company is claiming to have found the ultimate formula, but what they all have in common is a strong belief that the way to survive in today's harsh economic climate is to release the talents and creativity of the workforce and to solve problems as close as possible to the customer interface. Whether that is called delegation, empowerment, *hoshin* planning or simply passing decisions down the line is largely a question of semantics.

CASE STUDY – EMPOWERMENT AT RANK XEROX

Rank Xerox was formed in 1956 as a joint venture between Xerox Corporation of America and The Rank Organisation in the UK. It manufactures and markets document processing products and services throughout Europe, Asia and Africa and is known as *The Document Company*. All its products – fax machines, copiers, electronic printers and document imaging and management systems and software – add value to the four stages of the document life cycle: create, store and retrieve, distribute and print.

Rank Xerox (UK) Ltd was established in 1972 as the UK sales, marketing and support subsidiary of the international company, Rank Xerox Ltd. Headquartered at Uxbridge, it employs around 4,700 people in 50 locations and generates annual revenues approaching £500 million.

The joint venture had a dream start. It launched a revolutionary new product in 1959 which turned the company into a story-book success. At the time it was the fastest company in the world to reach a billion dollar turnover and it quickly became 'the darling of Wall Street', as Vernon Zelmer, the Canadian managing director of Rank Xerox UK puts it.

But in the early 1970s, the company's meteoric success was halted in its tracks. Its patents had started to run out and Japanese competition had entered the market with a vengeance. 'We had really taken our eye off the customer during this period of awesome growth,' recalls Zelmer. 'In 1979 our profits dropped from $1.2 billion to $600 million. Seventy-six per cent of new business in that year went to the competition, so we had some reason to take a look at what was happening to this company.'

Benchmarking

As part of the self-scrutiny, Rank Xerox adopted the technique of benchmarking, a continuous process of measuring its products, services and practices against leading competitors or those companies who are world renowned as leaders in a particular field. This helped the company to identify its strengths and weaknesses and to develop strategies to underline its strengths and eliminate areas of weakness. This provided it with the indicators it needed to meet its new corporate objective of achieving superiority in quality, product reliability and cost.

One of the first areas that Rank Xerox benchmarked was the productivity embedded in its long-range plan. Its productivity at the time was built on an eight per cent year on year compound growth rate. This compared very favourably with the average Western world company with a three per cent year on year productivity rate.

But when Rank Xerox benchmarked its best Japanese competitors it became clear it needed an 18 per cent compound growth rate over a five year period to bring it in line. A detailed look at leading Japanese competitors revealed some alarming shortfalls at Rank Xerox. It had nine times more production suppliers to the assembly line than the best Japanese competitors. It had seven times more product defects than the best competitors and at the bottom end of the market, the Japanese were selling their products at a lower price than Rank Xerox's manufacturing costs.

To catch up with the Japanese, Rank Xerox embarked on a paradigm shift in corporate policy in 1980 to transform the way it did business. This involved a series of critical steps that included benchmarking, employee involvement, leadership through quality and a general drive towards business excellence.

Employee Involvement

In the drive to higher levels of quality, Rank Xerox quickly recognised the importance of empowerment. It put in place a structured process called Policy Deployment, by which staff at all levels participated in influencing their work and their work life. Using this methodology, Rank Xerox was determined to ensure that the minds and talents of its people were applied fully and creatively to business problems and opportunities.

Leadership Through Quality
The model which has facilitated Rank Xerox's drive for quality is called *Leadership Through Quality* and was introduced in 1984. It has enabled Rank Xerox to achieve remarkable productivity results:

- Product and operations quality: It has reduced defects per hundred machines by ten times and achieved the industry benchmark
- Production suppliers have been reduced from 5,000 to 500
- Production line defects: Defective parts have been reduced from 4,000 parts per million to just 300 – an improvement of 13 times
- Improved supply quality has reduced the need for inspection of incoming goods to just five per cent.

The Payoff
These radical improvements have led to some significant dividends. For example, back in 1984 the company was losing one out of two major contracts it bid for. It currently only loses one out of 27 contracts. There have also been significant improvements in customer satisfaction. It has given Rank Xerox the confidence to introduce a total satisfaction guarantee, unique to its industry. It has set a target to achieve 100 per cent customer satisfaction during 1993.

To ensure that it remains a world class company, Rank Xerox has developed a business excellence model to keep the impetus going and drive the performance improvements forward. The model is built on six key pillars, two of which are management leadership and human resource management. Both are focused directly on the needs of the customer. The company's 12 operations in the UK are constantly required to evaluate themselves against these key elements of the business excellence model. Rank Xerox is convinced that to become world class in human resource management it needs to develop and empower its employees.

As a result of these self-examination exercises, Rank Xerox has arrived at a vision of the kind of company it wants to be and that vision has empowerment embedded in it. It has also helped Rank Xerox to set priorities and to reach a definite view of its purpose in life. Explains Zelmer:

Figure 11.1   Rank Xerox Empowerment Model

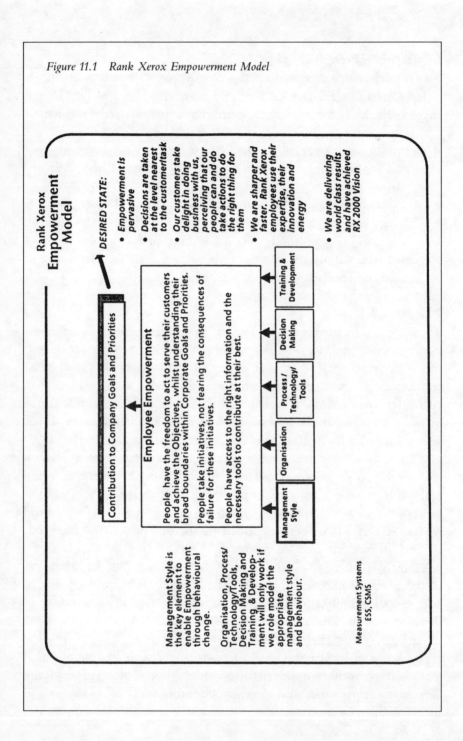

If you look at it from the customer point of view, the reason we exist is to provide document services which enhance productivity, so our purpose is to understand and anticipate customer document needs, to exceed their expectations and to be recognised as leaders in the use of innovative management practices. We will do that by being the leader in the global document market and by providing superior document technology. That's the vision.

The vision has been broadened into statements of corporate values which are built into the business plans and objectives of each part of the organisation.

The Empowerment Model

Empowerment is an integral part of the company goals and priorities required to achieve the world-class standards that Rank Xerox has set itself. In its empowerment model (see Figure 11.1), Rank Xerox defines its approach as the creation of an environment in which 'people have the freedom to act to serve their customers and achieve the objectives, whilst understanding their broad boundaries within corporate goals and priorities.' It adds that people need to be able to take initiatives without fearing the consequence of failure and that people need to have access to the right information and the necessary tools to contribute their best.

Rank Xerox has identified five important elements of empowerment:

- Management style
- Organisation
- Process/technology/tools
- Decision making
- Training and development

Explains Zelmer:

Empowerment is an easily misunderstood concept. We believe there are a number of enablers to make it happen. It isn't just delegation. We believe management style is critical. We believe the organisation

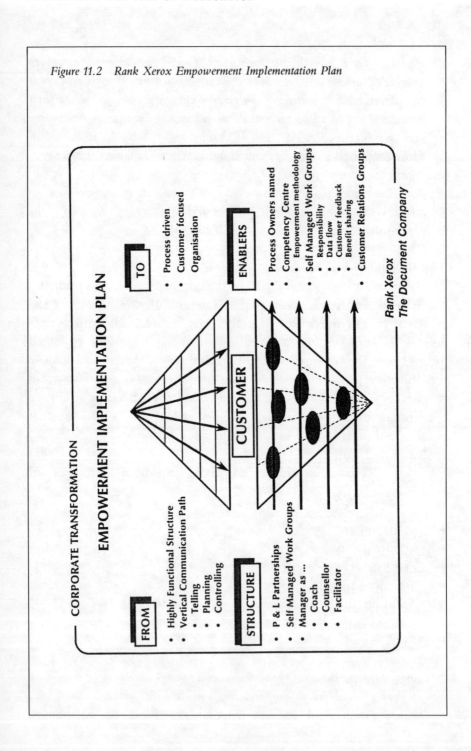

Figure 11.2   Rank Xerox Empowerment Implementation Plan

structure you're involved in is critical. We believe that the process and technology available to people dictates whether they're empowered or not. You can't be empowered these days if you're working with pen and pencil and the competition is working off lap-top computers.

The company has also identified a number of important elements necessary to achieve the ideal environment *for empowerment:*

- Empowerment is pervasive
- Decisions are taken at the level nearest the customer/task
- Our customers take delight in doing business with us, perceiving that our people can and do take actions to do the right thing for them
- We are sharper and faster. Rank Xerox employees use their expertise, their innovation and energy
- We are delivering world class results

Inverted pyramid

To achieve its customer focus and ensure that empowerment is exercised at the level nearest the interface with the customer, Rank Xerox has switched to an organisation structure that inverts its former pyramidal hierarchy (see Figure 11.2). In dispensing with the former command structure, Zelmer acknowledges that it was not without merit in the early stages of the company's history:

That was the organisation structure that made us the fastest company to a $1 billion turnover. In its day it was very successful. It actually pulled man out of the dark ages. But we learned very quickly when we benchmarked the Japanese that the companies which were starting to whip our backsides were those moving away from this. They were moving towards a process-driven, customer-focused organisation, so we tipped the pyramid upside down. The customer is at the top. We have a hundred thousand hearts and minds around the world focused on the customer. Our Number One objective is customer satisfaction and we will achieve it through an empowered organisation.

Managers are encouraged to operate cross-functionally within the inverted pyramid. This has led to the concept of regional partnerships. Explains Les Jones, Rank Xerox's human resources director in the UK:

> *A region used to be run by a mini-general manager with his sales, service and finance people reporting to him. Today, there is no mini-general manager. They run the business. Those three are equals. Everything happens when they all agree. They get paid the same. If they don't make the business, none of them get anything.*

In the same way, the company's training department is now run as a partnership. There is no longer a head of training. There are three managers who jointly run sales training, service training and management training as equal partners.

The regional partnerships have largely eradicated the conflict that used to exist between the functional managers under the old structure, according to Jones: 'There was always conflict because the sales manager and the finance manager and the service manager had conflicting priorities. Today there's very little conflict because they can't afford it. They'd all be a lot poorer as a result because we've put them under a common profit and loss account.'

Rank Xerox is also well down the road to turning its organisation into a mass of self-managed work groups (SMWGs). The company's entire customer service division has been converted into 250 SMWGs (see Chapter 10 on delegating on groups). The top managers in the service organisation have been switched from playing a command and control role to one of coaching, counselling and facilitating. A huge training programme has helped to achieve the transition.

Zelmer's ultimate aim is to eradicate functions altogether in Rank Xerox UK and focus on business processes laterally across the organisation. The intention is to fade out functional directors and replace them with directors of process:

> *Today we still have functional directors, but we have named process directors in every case for key processes, because as a customer you don't*

Figure 11.3   Role of the Manager

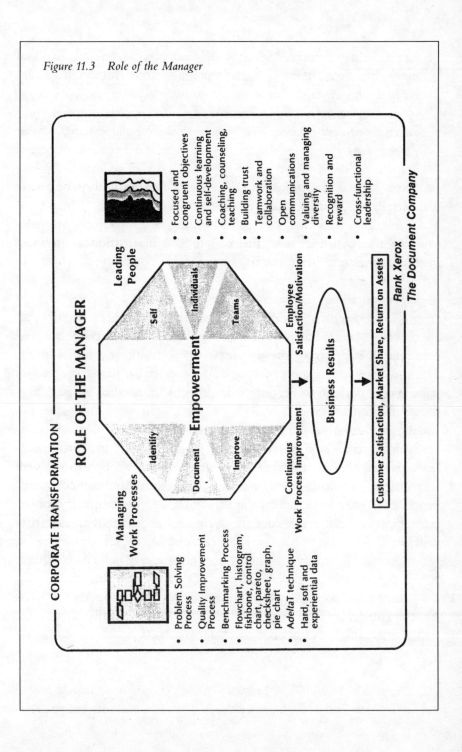

care about any particular function. All you want is for your product to move from sales, through manufacturing to service and billing. To facilitate this direction, we have put in place a process re-engineering competency centre within our systems organisation and have developed an empowerment methodology to help streamline the movement to a process focus.

Rank Xerox has found that the inverted pyramid structure has completely changed its strategic approach. Says Zelmer: 'When you make this kind of move, power and influence has to flow upwards towards the customer and the people at the customer interface instead of moving down the organisation.'

Management style

Clearly, management style has an important influence on the new approach. Managers need to act as facilitators, coaches and counsellors, supporting the development of teams and individuals. The company also expects managers to take risks, to challenge the *status quo* and remove barriers that prevent employees from using their full talents.

Rank Xerox sees managers in its empowered organisation performing two key functions – managing work processes and leading people (see Figure 11.3). The company's managers are responsible for flow-charting and documenting the actual work processes in their area and then applying the following quality tools, techniques and skills to reduce the cycle time and overall costs of the process:

- Problem solving skills
- Quality improvement techniques
- Benchmarking
- The use of statistical tools such as A delta T

Rank Xerox managers are responsible for empowering employees through:

- Focused and congruent objectives
- Continuous learning and self-development
- Coaching, counselling and teaching
- Building trust
- Teamwork and collaboration
- Open communications
- Valuing and managing diversity
- Recognition and reward
- Cross-functional leadership

Summing up, Zelmer points out that Rank Xerox managers are responsible for 'moving us to a future state that is more desirable through managing work processes and empowering people to yield better business results. We absolutely drive that concept into our managers on our training courses.'

The process starts even earlier; every new recruit to the company receives a booklet which sets out the way Rank Xerox works and the values and principles it holds most dear. It details work and quality processes and how to work in teams and groups. It includes problem-solving techniques, elementary statistical tools and the benchmarking process.

Proof of the Pudding

What evidence is there that empowerment has taken hold at Rank Xerox? Zelmer is in no doubt that it has become the accepted way of life among the vast majority of employees. A company survey revealed that 67 per cent of the employees were satisfied with the amount of empowerment they enjoyed. Zelmer is convinced that there has been a substantial rise in that percentage since the survey was undertaken. 'It's too soon to declare an ultimate home-run victory, but there's nothing on the horizon that would lead us to doubt it. I haven't met an individual who doesn't agree with the direction.'

Many of the employees who were initially sceptical about the new approach are steadily being won over, according to Jones, even though the reasons may not be entirely altruistic:

> *I guess they saw simple choices two or three years ago – survival for the business and themselves and bringing it back into real growth and profitability, or the alternative, which was not very encouraging with the recession as it was then around the corner. So they have made the transition in the main and I think they are very enthusiastic about the future and the fact that change isn't necessarily bad.*

The company will continue to measure the effectiveness of empowerment, however. All managers are obliged to conduct a management practices survey among the employees reporting to them each year and a number of the questions relate to empowerment.

Where Next?

Rank Xerox has clearly come a long way – from the bureaucracy of the 1960s to what Zelmer describes as 'the dynamic, cross-functional, customer-oriented, self-managed, empowered organisation of the 90s. But the real leading edge thinkers today say that the end point is the network organisation.'

The company is already some way down that road. It has a number of networks comprising managers with common interests within the company and several networks jointly made up of Rank Xerox managers and suppliers and customers. Internally, for example, there is a network of 21 quality managers who meet regularly to examine common issues. Externally there is a network of 90 concessionaires who represent Rank Xerox in the outside world.

But Zelmer is cautious about moving towards an organisation that is totally dominated by networks. The risks involved are obvious. An organisation that has little or no control mechanisms can be as ineffective as one that is over-supervised. 'It's the next step theoretically, but we must walk before we run,' he says warily.

Jones is equally cautious: 'I absolutely hate the thought of revolution, yet there is a degree of impatience within any organisation to move faster than is perhaps appropriate. If it's going to be lasting and really stick and become a way of life, then evolution is the route. Most revolutions don't last – even the Russian one.'

There is a preliminary step that needs to be taken prior to attempting to become a network organisation, in the opinion of Jones:

> We need to understand what is the core company we need to run the business with in future. At the moment we have a very large company with a lot of activity that is not central to our future needs. You can sub-contract, buy-in, use external expertise a lot more effectively than we do at present.

Employer of choice?

Hand in hand with the changes in structure and management style, Rank Xerox has been addressing the issue of how it can attract the most suitable people to work for it to make the empowered organisation a reality. Jones explains:

> It's no news to anybody that what we've called the second industrial revolution is beginning to happen – leaner organisations, flatter structures and so on. Our response to that was to take our organisation from where we were to become the employer of choice – the name people want on their CVs. To do that we had to start thinking about what sort of images and values we wanted to market as a business. In the same way that we market products, we saw the need to market ourselves to the labour market.

The company identified a whole range of qualities and issues that it wanted to be associated with in order to attract the best employees. These included team working in a non-status environment, self-fulfilment, empowerment, entrepreneurial spirit and a share of value creation. Jones concludes:

To support that, we asked what sort of people the 90s employees were going to be. What are they going to want out of life? Some of the things we think they are going to want are role enrichment, recognition, loyalty to project skills not businesses and so on. That is all supporting the drive to empowerment.

Figure 11.4 Elements of empowerment: management style

ATTRIBUTES

From	To
• Managers operate tight command and control, limiting groups and individuals, capacity to act quickly and effectively to internal and external customer requirements	• Managers act as facilitators, coaches and counsellors supporting the development of the team and the individual to act quickly and effectively towards their internal and external customers
• Managers do not take risks, maintain the status quo and act on internal requirements	• Managers take risks, challenge the status quo, remove barriers in the interest of increasing people's capacity to act productively and towards the customer
• Managers define the objectives, the actions and their way of achieving actions and are focused on results	• Managers work collaboratively with their team to define objects actions processes and customers; their focus is on supporting improvement towards results and developing the team and individuals, capacity to act
• Managers recognise people only for results	• Managers recognise and reward people for innovation, process improvement and results
• Managers do not accept failure and use fear to control	• Managers recognise and reward people's right to be wrong, and drive out fear.

Figure 11.5 Elements of empowerment: organisation

ATTRIBUTES

From	To
→	• Xerox 2000
• Hierarchical, functional with many levels and small spans of control	• Flat, process orientated with broad span of control
• Internally focused, based on command and control limiting the capacity of individuals to act	• External focus based on the needs of customer and market and maximising individual capacity to act
• Concerned with only Rank Xerox	• Extended focus beyond RX to incorporate partnership with suppliers, concessionaire and customers
• Managed non-autonomous work groups	• Autonomous self-managing groups
	• Partnerships/External contact and relation based

Figure 11.6 Elements of empowerment: process/technology/tools

ATTRIBUTES

From

- Processes are not always understood, improvement exists but simplification is uncommon

- Processes are seen to be, or are bureaucratic, or not used; fire fighting is common

- Technology and systems do not always support or are unavailable to users.

- Technology and systems not seen as user friendly or flexible

To

- Processes are understood, improved/simplified by those that use them in the interest of productivity and the customer.

- Processes do not impede creativity/innovation but support by liberating the time and energy of people from constant fire fighting. They provide the means by which people can work productively together to deliver output and flexible response

- Technology and systems are available to directly support processes and people in performing their work

- Technology and systems are user friendly, integrated and capable of being easily improved. The user is directly involved in specification and improvement.

Figure 11.7 Elements of empowerment: decision making

ATTRIBUTES

From	To
• Decisions are deferred up the organisational hierarchy	• Decisions are devolved to be nearest to the customer/task resulting in ownership, productivity and responsiveness
• We do not understand what we mean by empowerment, we recognise what we do as task delegation. It is often fragmented and not seen as process, little technology support is provided	• We train people, give them the processes and the technology, they are then able to make the best decisions, at the time these are needed.
• Only senior people are equipped to make decisions, however in order to do so they must be given information and facts by their staff. Delays are built in as a consequence, business is lost and staff and customers suffer frustration	• Devolution of decision making has increased productivity very significantly, our customer satisfaction results have improved, through employees responding to customer requirements as they are raised
• Senior people are slowly understanding their role as facilitators, in many cases there is a lack of skill to carry it out and also a disinclination to learn and adapt	• Effective Teamworking and management facilitation is standard practice. This has demonstrated that direct control of staff is not necessary to good productivity and performance. Individuals and teams understand and own their boundaries and capabilities. Policy Deployment is used as a key tool to formalise boundaries

---

Figure 11.8   Elements of empowerment: training and development

ATTRIBUTES	
From	**To**
• Training and Development does not incorporate Empowerment but supports a command and control style	• Training and Development supports the Empowerment Desired State with the concept and practice fully integrated
• Little understanding about how to train and develop managers to be Empowered	• Clear ways developed and implemented to support the change in management style including core competence in facilitating, coaching and counselling
• Development based on classroom training	• Managers able to provide and lead the development of Empowerment in others through style (role modelling, facilitating. coaching & counselling)

CASE STUDY – *HOSHIN* PLANNING AT HEWLETT-PACKARD

Empowerment is not a widely used term at Hewlett-Packard. The company is, however, attempting to devolve an increasing amount of authority to its employees within a clearly defined framework that involves a detailed planning process allied to performance evaluation and a tailor-made form of management by objectives. This is backed up by self-development which aims to give every employee the opportunity to enhance their skills and plan their careers. The computer company believes that it is vital that its employees should have clear-cut guidelines within which to operate, but that within those guidelines they should be given the freedom to achieve their individual goals with the minimum of intervention from senior management. Indeed, the company increasingly sees senior management becoming 'the servant' of the employees in its concept of devolved authority. It has also delegated responsibility to individual employees to develop their own skills since it believes that the individual is best placed to know what knowledge and abilities he or she will require to fulfil future career goals.

Hewlett-Packard is an international company manufacturing electronic measurement and computation equipment, including computers, heart-monitoring devices and computer peripherals. It employs some 90,000 people around the world – 4,000 of them in the UK – and generates an annual turnover of around $17 billion.

The company operates a matrix management structure and while it encourages a high level of autonomy in each country, it controls a number of functions internationally. For example, research and development is managed centrally. This is to avoid the strong risk of 're-inventing the wheel', as one Hewlett-Packard manager puts it, and to contain R&D costs, which amount to about ten per cent of the company's total revenues.

The computer industry has been experiencing hard times in recent years – a conbination of the industry reaching some maturity and a global recession among previously booming economies. The trend in the industry has been to produce ever more high performance equipment while dramatically reducing the price to the customer. This, coupled with the recession, has put Hewlett-Packard under pressure to reduce costs and improve efficiency. These adverse trends have created a climate in which control and monitoring are essential for survival, while at the same time the company has been anxious to devolve responsibility to those closest to the customer interface. This has created something of a dichotomy of purpose. Managing this ambivalence represents an interesting challenge for Hewlett-Packard. Mike Haffenden, director of personnel at Hewlett-Packard's Bracknell-based UK headquarters, explains: 'On the one hand, you need to create an environment that allows people to innovate, yet, on the other hand, has the disciplines which control costs and the disciplines to ensure that we get products to market very quickly.'

Normally, for example research workers in a company like Hewlett-Packard are normally given a high degree of freedom to operate creatively. It is the area in most companies where people are allowed to do their own thing and pursue their own ideas with the minimum of interference. Hewlett-Packard recognises that there has to be an element of latitude, but at the same time it believes that in the current economic climate there has to be structure and discipline. 'If you can't raise your prices, if you can't sell more, the only real element of retaining your profits is controlling and reducing costs', says Haffenden. 'At the same time, the speed of getting the products to market dominates people's attention in Hewlett-Packard.'

Core competencies

All these pressures from the market-place have caused a lot of soul-searching at Hewlett-Packard and prompted the company to re-evaluate its operating methods and its future priorities. Haffenden describes the process:

> A big thrust at the moment is looking at what we do – what are our core competencies? Where are our areas of high added value? From the organisation structure perspective, we are not the traditional pyramid you might see in many companies. Our shape is much more like a diamond where we sub-contract various functions at the bottom end to other organisations. We don't do our own catering on this site; we don't do our own security; we don't have our own travel bureau; we don't have our own temporary staff agency. We sub-contract; we get somebody else to do it. We are now looking at extending that into other areas. It is completely changing the organisation design for us.

More Fluid Communication

The changing climate has prompted Hewlett-Packard to re-evaluate its personnel policies as well. It is considering dispensing with job evaluation. It currently has around 13 job grades, but Haffenden feels they are no longer applicable to the way the company operates. Such segregation is not compatible with a much flatter organisation structure and a desire for more fluid forms of communication up and down the organisation. Haffenden sees the need for 'fewer lines of communication, minimised organisational barriers, less hierarchy. People have got to get on and take their own decisions.'

In place of the old hierarchical systems, Hewlett-Packard has put in place systems that involve the entire workforce in a process of detailed planning. 'Many organisations have management by objectives. We have it coming out of our ears and we link it to quality much more than most organisations do. So planning is part of our quality process,' explains Haffenden.

Hoshin Plans

As part of this intense planning process, each department in the organisation is required to produce *hoshin* plans, a technique borrowed from the Japanese. *Hoshin* plans concentrate on breakthrough issues that are going to drive the business forward. Every department has its general plans which need to be fulfilled in order to ensure future progress, but *hoshin* plans attempt to isolate those issues which can help the organisation to make a quantum leap forward and add significantly to the value of the business, particularly when meeting customers' specific needs. A rigorous follow-up process ensures progress is measured at regular intervals. When a *hoshin* plan needs more resources or a different approach, action is taken swiftly to ensure that it does not die on the vine.

The plans provide the guidelines for Hewlett-Packard employees. It tells them what is expected of them. How the goals are achieved is entirely up to them – the company is primarily interested in results.

The plans are regularly reviewed and senior management acts as a resource providing any additional needs. This can be in the form of extra resources or advice on how to change the approach when obstacles appear to be blocking progress. Allan James, employee relations manager, stresses the importance of adapting the plans to changing circumstances and not allowing them to be cast in tablets of stone: 'When you get into the nitty-gritty of making plans happen, you come across barriers that may be unexpected. The process involves taking those into account and changing the plans or re-assigning priorities.'

In 1992 the personnel department had two *hoshin* plans, for example. One concerned applying quality methods to personnel issues. The other was to do with helping the organisation to be more flexible by 'giving it policies and procedures on the human resource management side which encourage flexibility rather than discourage it,' as James puts it. For example, the personnel department was charged with providing line managers with analytical tools to carry out performance management more effectively:

> *The planning processes that we are interested in are those that try to achieve clarity of purpose and direction, but leave the choices to the people who are committed to them. It's really about creating clarity of purpose, getting commitment to that purpose through a participative process and then giving everyone the freedom to decide how they go about it. Management then needs to be able to measure what's going on to get good feedback and to ascertain whether the plan is on track or off track and literally act as a servant to the team in terms of any additional resources that are needed.*

Self-Development

With greater responsibility falling on employees further down the line, Hewlett-Packard has inevitably given a lot of thought about how to equip them with the skills to cope. The company encourages employees to enhance their skills through a programme of self-development and life-long learning. Elaborates Haffenden:

> *We believe very much that individuals are responsible for their own development. Everybody says that and then they don't articulate it any further. We have a thrust that says to people: self-development is development of yourself by yourself. Many people talk about allying training delivery to business needs. That's an idea of the 1970s, because these days things are changing so quickly. You have got to help people*

with personal growth because you don't know what tomorrow's business needs are going to be. You've got to develop people as individuals. You change your boss every three years anyway. Unless you do it for yourself, the chances are it's not going to happen.

There are several elements to Hewlett-Packard's approach to self-development. The starting point is a self-development workshop open to all employees interested in exploring career advancement. The workshop looks at the way careers are developing in the 1990s and at the end of each session participants come away with a personal plan on how to advance their own career. In tandem with this, coaching workshops are held that encourage managers to create an environment in which individuals can develop themselves.

A third element is an electronic mail advertising scheme that keeps employees informed of job opportunities throughout the worldwide organisation. In addition, they are provided with what the company calls 'road maps' giving them an indication of the route they need to take in order to fulfil their aspirations for higher level jobs. All this is backed up by learning centres established throughout the organisation where employees, setting their own pace and acting on their own initiative, can acquire whatever skills they require, from technical skills through to managerial training. It is even possible to take an MBA at one of the centres.

In conjunction with this multi-faceted self-development programme, employees are instructed in the principles of life-long learning. They become conversant with different learning styles and are taught to draw up 'interest inventories' to pinpoint the directions their careers might take. Among many other techniques, a network analysis planner helps them to discover if they are making contacts with the necessary people in the organisation to facilitate good networking.

An Integrated Approach

Hewlett-Packard has adopted an integrated approach in which employees plan their careers at the self-development workshops and decide specifically what skills they need to acquire to achieve their personal goals. They are then given the opportunity to develop those skills at the learning centres provided. Performance evaluation provides the opportunity to review their personal career goals and check whether they are on course. Performance evaluations are carried out from several different perspectives, taking in the views of senior management, subordinates and customers. An attempt to include peer evaluation was abandoned because it proved impractical.

Performance evaluation is based very much on key result areas. It does not deal with more esoteric areas such as communications and decision-making, nor does it include judgements about a person's ability to delegate. Says Haffenden: 'All these things are very difficult to define and very difficult to measure. It's the results that are important.'

One result is that Hewlett-Packard employees are motivated to take on responsibilities that fall outside their formal job description – reinforcing the view that job evaluation is a redundant process. For example, a secretary runs the Learning Centre at Hewlett-Packard's Bracknell office. Haffenden's secretary is responsible for organising the allocation of £1 million worth of equipment a year to universities and other education/ research establishments in the UK under the company's Strategic Equipment Grants Programme.

Other examples abound in the company's total quality control programme. Employees at all levels are involved in TQC task forces. Summarising the Hewlett-Packard approach, Haffenden knits it all together:

This is what we have to do; these are the people responsible for doing it; your performance will be monitored by performance evaluation; you are responsible for your own development; and the processes and procedures that we will use to get things done will be consistent with TQC.

This may seem a very systemised approach in the age of empowerment, but Hewlett-Packard has clearly reached the view that delegating responsibility down the line without providing the framework to establish the boundaries of authority and a sense of cohesive purpose would be inviting disaster at a time of economic stringency and fierce competition in the market-place.

Allan James describes it as largely:

a move from organisational control to self-control within a structured environment. If you paint a clear picture for people of what it is you are trying to achieve and buy them into that process, they are more likely to be able to work out for themselves how to get there. Then the issue of motivation and delegation in one sense becomes easy, because people are self-determining, particularly when you move into the professional levels.

There is an argument that the more structured the guidelines are the more comfortable managers feel about delegating to employees down the line. If the boundaries of authority are vague, employees are hesitant about taking personal initiatives and the senior manager is nervous about delegating authority to someone who might exceed the limits of his responsibility.

James draws an analogy with ship navigation:

When I was at college we were always told that it was the manager who made the decisions and steered the ship, whereas these days you've got sophisticated data telling you the directional heading and it is not necessary for the captain to turn the wheel. The individual can read the data and knows what it means. All you've got to do is be very clear about the fact you are heading for Africa rather than South America.

CASE STUDY – A FRAMEWORK FOR INITIATIVE AT W.H. SMITH

Leadership skills have always been high on the agenda at W.H. Smith, the widely dispersed retail chain. Some 3,500 managers and staff pass through its group training centre at Abingdon in Berkshire every year and about a third of the skills that they learn are related to leadership. 'We recognise that we are managing a dispersed organisation – 1,500 units on the ground – and that most of our managers are charged with getting the best that they can from the people that work with them. Leadership has a key part to play in that,' notes Rodney Buse, W.H. Smith's group personnel director.

In the past two years the company has been taking a new look at exactly how it wants its businesses to operate. It has launched a programme of cultural change that is aiming to switch from a command and control management style to one where the individual businesses decide their own destiny within a clearly defined framework. The businesses themselves are being encouraged to pass more authority down the line to the employees closest to the customer. The new approach is about as far as you can get from the old-style management principles of Frederick Taylor, which promoted the belief that senior managers have all the answers and that their prime function is to parcel out tasks to employees who are incapable of having ideas of their own.

Buse quotes the views of a leading Japanese industrialist to emphasise how inappropriate the Taylor model has become:

> *We are going to win and the West is going to lose out. There's not much you can do about it because the reasons for your failure are within yourselves. Your firms are built on the Taylor model. Even worse, so are your heads, with your bosses doing the thinking while the workers wield the screwdrivers. You are convinced deep down that this is the right way to run a business. For you the essence of management is getting the ideas out of the heads of the bosses and into the hands of labour. We are beyond the Taylor model. Business, we know, is now complex and difficult, the survival of firms so hazardous in an environment increaingly unpredictable, competitive and fraught with danger, that their continued existence depends on the day-to-day mobilisation of every ounce of intelligence.*

An Alternative Style

Such a stark condemnation of the way many companies are still run in the West is a good starting point for examining how to adapt leadership styles for the modern business environment. It is one thing to eschew Taylor. It is another to find an alternative management style that fits the modern era and will prove the pessimists wrong. Buse is among those who firmly believe that the Taylorian model is totally inappropriate in today's complex business environment:

> *Very early on in my career it was possible to know all the jobs in a department and therefore to be totally involved and to have the answers to very many issues. Today that's not possible. IT more than anything else has changed that. The ability of somebody at the top to have a finger on everything that is happening in an organisation is pushing all our skills to the absolute extreme. Therefore, you have to work on a model that says good ideas can be anywhere.*

Creating an environment in which all its employees can contribute their skills and imaginations is the task that W.H. Smith is currently engaged in. But developing a climate in which everyone is free to take individual initiatives also has its dangers: Buse emphasises the need to establish a framework of guidelines that ensure employees do not deviate from imperative corporate goals. He quotes a simple example:

> *A W.H. Smith retail branch cannot sell Coca-Cola, because we don't sell soft drinks. Therefore, a very enabled manager in Skegness, thinking that he can increase sales trying to sell Coca-Cola, will be in breach of our framework. The clarity of the boundaries is absolutely essential.*

To tackle this issue, the company began by asking its directors at the very top of the organisation where they would place the boundaries. In particular, it has attempted to establish what the boundaries of responsibility should be between the corporate centre and the businesses in the field and what mechanisms should be applied to ensure that the limits are understood and complied with.

A Table of Responsibilities
Out of this exercise a table of responsibilities has emerged. The centre's expected involvement in decision-making is specified against

a list of sample responsibilities. The table specifies when the centre would expect to make an outright decision, when it might merely comment and when it would expect to 'vigorously challenge' a decision made by one of the businesses. The table also illustrates the kind of situations in which the central coaching team would expect to arbitrate between two or more of the businesses. An obvious example would be when two of the businesses interpret corporate policy differently and risk causing confusion in the market place.

For example, if W.H. Smith Group was about to launch a new retail concept with a new brand name, the centre would expect to be heavily involved in the decision-making. On the other hand, the central coaching team would only comment in the event of a shopfloor worker adopting an unusual style of dress. It could not insist that the employee change his or her mode of dress. That would be a matter for local management. Similarly, the centre is only expected to comment on issues to do with product quality. 'We are running a number of brands within the group and those brands are unique to those businesses. Waterstone's will be run differently from Our Price Music, which will be run differently from W.H. Smith Retail. It's important to that brand that its individuality is maintained,' explains Buse.

However, the corporate centre is likely to challenge vigorously a decision by one of its retail chains to site a new outlet in a town where there are already a number of W.H. Smith Group businesses in operation. Buse describes 'a vigorous challenge' as meaning that 'at the end of the day the centre cannot decide, but it can ask a business to justify what it is doing. If the power of the argument is strong enough, then the case stands. If the power of the argument is not strong, it should be made clear to one and all that it does not stand the test.'

The centre acts as arbiter only when various parties within the group fail to reach an agreement, about shared resources, for example. It might concern the use of a corporate facility such as the group training centre. Similarly, if one of the businesses wants to change its employment package and that is likely to have a knock-on effect on other businesses in the group, the centre will step in to arbitrate.

The individual businesses are being encouraged to adopt a similar approach within their own organisation, in the hope that the new culture will be cascaded down to branch level. In keeping with the more widely dispersed authority, the company is not imposing the system on the managers of its businesses. They have the freedom to choose to what extent they wish to embrace the new style and at what pace. Buse is anxious to avoid any impression that there is any compulsion: 'What you lose then are the ideas and the concepts and what you end up with are rules and regulations. We are trying to avoid that at all costs. What we are trying to do is communicate it and it is as much attitudinal as it is physical.'

Coaching Skills

To reinforce the new approach, senior management courses on coaching skills are being run at the group training centre. This has become essential in the light of the new role corporate management is expected to play. The function of the centre is now not to act as policemen but to coach others in the organisation to share skills and develop knowledge.

The groundwork for introducing the new culture had already been carried out. David Marchant, group training manager, points out that prior to establishing the table of responsibilities, an increasing amount of authority had been devolved to the businesses. 'So each head of a business – W.H. Smith Retail, News, Our Price Music – has been delegated the authority to run the business as they see fit. This was trying to outline the relationship that they should have with the centre and the areas on which they should refer to the centre for guidance or expert direction.'

Adds Buse: 'We have tried very hard not to hype or oversell – or indeed sell at all – what's going on, but if a director wants to live the words, if you like, then his managers will role model rather than saying "this is the way of doing things" and people not being able to marry the words with the music.'

The group training centre is reinforcing this supportive approach with courses in team-building and action learning, as well as leadership. It is also steering the company towards becoming a learning organisation. Running through all the training is a central aim to promote core principles at the root of the new approach – directness, openness to ideas, commitment to the success of others, willingness to accept personal accountability and a strong sense of team work. An overriding thrust is the delegation of responsibility and authority to the levels nearest to the products and the customers. These are the principles that Buse believes will drive the programme forward.

Little Resistance

Buse is optimistic about the number of people who are likely to accept the new culture. He is a strong believer in the 5-90-5 principle. He anticipates that five per cent of the employees will willingly embrace it; ninety per cent will want convincing, but will adopt it when they see it working for them; and that five per cent will decide it's not for them. The latter will probably decide for themselves to leave the company. But the need for a framework within which to operate the new style is paramount in Buse's view:

> *If you enable people and don't discipline them all the time and you are not acting as a policeman all the time, they can very quickly become totally disruptive to themselves and to the organisation unless they can work within a framework. So, whereas under the Taylor model you can cope with people who do not follow the company line, under this model you can't. They usually decide for themselves that the organisation is not right for them, but I don't believe the numbers (of dissenters) should be enormous and I do believe it is self-selecting.*

Marchant believes that managers will need to take a number of key factors into account when delegating within the new culture:

> *The person who is doing the delegating needs to make good judgements about what to delegate and to which people he can delegate. The sort of things he or she should consider are: what is their skill, what is the nature of the task and do they have all the support they need?*

Upward Aspects of Delegation

The upward aspect of delegation is also something that Marchant would like to see encouraged. Subordinates should consider it quite normal to approach their senior managers offering to take on a project for which they believe they have the necessary skills. 'That's one of the elements that is often ignored, especially in an organisation that is quite hierarchical traditionally, where people aren't used to volunteering for things or taking responsibility.'

Marchant suggests that employees will grow in confidence about volunteering for tasks when they are praised for work competently carried out. Senior managers should encourage them to come back for more.

The delegation process runs more smoothly, in Buse's view, when the subordinate keeps his senior manager informed purely about those matters that satisfy him the project is going well. The system falls down when the senior manager has to keep on inquiring about what is happening when things go wrong.

Delegation requires of the individual to whom the power and the authority has been delegated to keep their immediate supervisor advised of those few events that are critical. If that isn't done, the boss will interfere. Many people cry out for further delegation. What they don't understand is the other side of the coin. The person being delegated to has a contract to make sure his or her boss knows sufficient of what is going on to maintain the right level of trust.

New Approach to Recruitment

The culture change at W.H. Smith has prompted it to review its approach to recruitment and succession planning. It recognises that certain people are likely to be more attuned to the new management style than others. It is attempting to understand more fully the personality traits of the people who are most likely to be successful in the new environment. It is seeking to understand, for example, what makes good coaches or skilled delegators. Why do certain people choose to delegate more than others? All these issues are having a major impact on recruitment policies. Says Buse:

We are trying to isolate the traits of people who will want to identify with this way of working. The big difficulty, particularly when you are operating in a difficult climate, is for people to believe that the task is better achieved through the new processes. They argue that the only way to get the task done is through the old methods.

Finding the people who will resist that idea could be critical to the success of the culture change programme. What W.H. Smith Group is seeking above all else are leaders as opposed to managers. Buse draws the distinction:

A good manager can describe exactly how a task should be done and a good leader can describe very powerfully what needs to be done – what the result should be. Delegation comes very much from those leadership principles. If I can describe to you well enough what the outcome needs to be, then I can enable you to take the key decisions. You know best how to arrive at the answer because you are closest to the issue. Therefore a leader is more capable of promoting delegation skills than a manager who does it in a very controlled manner.

A Vision of the Future

The main thrust of W.H. Smith's attempted culture change focuses on the need to recognise that the leadership styles that predominated in past decades under-utilised the talents and capabilities of employees. Sir Malcolm Field, the company's group managing director, has a clear vision of the paradigm shift that needs to be made to harness these skills for the good of all concerned:

In the last decade in particular, there have been significant improvements in the development of skills and educational standards within the work force, which means the need to change relationships and attitudes towards employees . . . Employees want to be part of the group, but at the same time they want to distinguish themselves within the group and they want to be to a greater extent now in control of their own destiny. Thus the needs of the market and the individual employees seem to point in the same direction, creating a visible and inspiring purpose, enabling front-

line employees to pursue this purpose with all their talents and energies and it is with these elements of the new vision that I particularly want our staff in W.H. Smith to work.

It will take several more years before the company can feel confident the new culture has taken hold. Comments Buse:

You can measure input and you can measure output. It's far less easy to measure outcome and even more difficult to measure the impact. However, we've had some groups that have been working together for a year where the accountant on the team can point to quantifiable benefits as a result of a better working relationship. It is difficult to say to what extent that can be measured, but I have no doubt it can lead to a more effective way of businesses operating. Internal and external attitudinal work will provide the evidence, but ultimately it will be the verdict of the customer that will finally decide on the value that these processes deliver.

CASE STUDY – OPEN STYLE AT COW & GATE

When Peter Roebuck, a former Unilever executive, took over in 1989 as managing director of Cow & Gate, the Wiltshire-based baby foods and clinical nutrition company, he found an organisation that was embedded in a traditional operating style unsuited to an increasingly competitive environment. Many of its managers were long-serving; its location in rural Wiltshire and the nature of its products fostered a climate of inertia and complacency. A contributory factor was the fact that the sensitivity of the relationship between mother and baby is not something that encourages dramatic swings and changes. An atmosphere prevailed in which it was comfortable to do things the way they had always been done. It soon became obvious to Roebuck that a major change of culture was needed at Cow & Gate, but it was not immediately obvious how this should be brought about:

People were doing an adequate job, doing things reasonably well in the ways they had always done them in a market they had always been in. Therefore, the whole process of change was not only alien to the business itself, it was something the existing managers clearly weren't equipped to handle.

But however traumatic the process might have to be, Roebuck was convinced that a new approach was vital for the development of the business:

Change in the outside market place was happening so fast that there was no way any business could stand still and ignore it. If you do stand by and ignore it, eventually the business will decline and with it job opportunities. If you are a fairly stable business, a fairly profitable business with a good market share, you can survive longer than those who are more fragile, but at the end of the day you are going to lose.

Another impediment to progress that Roebuck recognised soon after his arrival was a fraught relationship between the Wiltshire firm and its Dutch parent group, Nutricia. The Dutch dairy products group had acquired Cow & Gate from Unigate in 1981, but after a brief honeymoon period the two companies clashed over the way they should operate together. When Roebuck took over, Cow & Gate was still resisting any attempt by Nutricia to get it to become more receptive to different ways of doing things. It was clear to Roebuck that relations with the Dutch would have to be repaired before any programme of cultural change could be introduced at Cow & Gate: 'The relationship we had with the Dutch was actually impeding us in our development when it should have been enhancing it; we should have been gaining from being part of the group, not losing.'

Contamination Scare
However, three months after he took over, Roebuck found himself immersed in a major crisis that overshadowed all the other problems. A blackmailer was threatening to contaminate jars of Heinz baby foods, which led to a spate of hoaxes affecting the industry as a

whole. Cow & Gate had no option but to remove its baby food products from the shelves. The scare did not affect the company's baby milks products, the bedrock of its business, but it did temporarily destroy its baby food market and threaten to wipe out its factory in Wells, in Somerset, employing 240 people.

For about four months turnover from the baby foods business disappeared completely. It hit the company's bottom line to the tune of several million pounds. However, Cow & Gate came through the crisis, slowly built the baby foods business up again and even managed eventually to expand its market share. This in turn helped the Wiltshire company restore its relationship with Nutricia, which was impressed with how the crisis was handled.

It was the kind of cataclysmic event that could be a useful springboard for change, but after the dust had settled, Roebuck was left with the impression that he had an even greater uphill task than he had imagined:

> Strangely enough, it reinforced some of the feelings I had about the complacency that was around. We had this major catastrophe that hit our bottom line enormously and people behaved as if it would go away and life would return to normal. The fact that this enormous event, which had every significance you could think of, didn't seem to shake the very foundations of the company, was something that was probably most telling.

No Time for Evolution

It left Roebuck with the conviction that he had to do something 'fairly significant and fairly substantial' and that the change process could not be evolutionary. He was also convinced that some of the management would have to be replaced in order to make a cultural change work. A number of senior managers left the business.

There was no pressure on Cow & Gate to change its operating style to cope with a deteriorating market. In fact, the company was by then in a position of considerable strength. It had come through a serious crisis; it had repaired its relationship with its parent group; it had completed the initial development of a third leg to its business – a clinical nutrition product range; and it had achieved new levels of profitability that augured well for the future.

In addition, a focus on cost awareness had been introduced that emphasised that although the company was providing an important community service, its future survival depended on a good level of profitability.

All these improvements had primarily been driven from the top. The question Roebuck now faced was: 'How do I get the rest of the business to feel this same sense of drive – this same requirement to question, to look at, to want to do things? How can I get 400 people rather than just ten or so moving the whole thing forward?' The answer, quite plainly, was to change the culture of the business. The only alternative would have been to change many more people in the company, but that was clearly impractical and undesirable.

Everyday Initiatives

What was needed was a change of climate in which people in the company felt they could take initiatives to make improvements in their everyday work. They had to be persuaded that such initiatives were welcomed and managers, who had grown accustomed over many years to a comfortable, stable environment, had to be prevailed upon to encourage their subordinates to challenge the way things had always been done. Essentially, a way had to be found for employees to feel confident about taking quality and service initiatives, which might seem minor when viewed singly, but which would add up to a major shift in attitudes and contribution. Roebuck elaborates:

We had done most of the major changes. We now needed to get to the medium and smaller-sized changes, which are about people in their every day business seeing the things that can be improved, actually looking for them – trying to get that sort of spirit. But how do you do it? We came to the conclusion that what we had to do first and foremost was create an environment that enabled people to feel comfortable to take on these quality and service initiatives.

To achieve this, Roebuck did not see any need to tamper with the company's organisation structure. It was not organisational constraints that were holding people back in his view. It was the absence of a climate that encouraged personal initiatives:

> *It wasn't that people were banging up against the structure and therefore in order to empower them you needed to be able to give them more authority, because they were thrusting to get through these corporate boundaries which were holding them in. They weren't thrusting to get through at all. People could have done lots of things to test the system, but few did.*

Roebuck argues that working within the bounds of some kind of authority is inescapable:

> *We all have to live with authority in some way or other. Whether you do it within the business, you have to do it in the outside world. We have to do it with our parent company. There is no place at which authority finishes. We are saying to people that they should be prepared to work within the bounds of authority, but that they should challenge authority. They should find out who has the authority and persuade that person to let them make the improvements they see necessary. Eliminating authority and working without any structure would be chaos.*

An example of what Roebuck is aiming at is an initiative that has been taken by the receptionists at Cow & Gate's head office near Trowbridge. Examining how they could provide a better service to both outside callers and internal staff, they went around to every department in the company finding out precisely what responsibilities everyone had. From that information, they have drawn up a manual that helps them to direct callers to the right person when the caller does not have a specific contact in the company.

An Environment of Continuous Improvement
The company calls the new approach an *Open Style* culture. It defines it as:

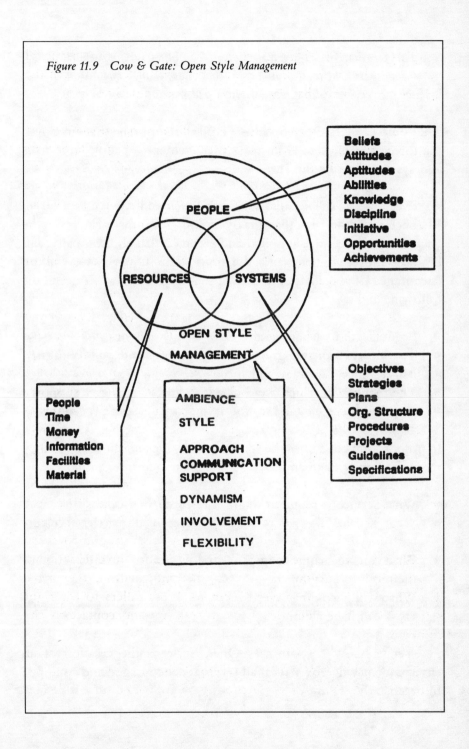

Figure 11.9   Cow & Gate: Open Style Management

The creation of an environment of continuous improvement which encourages: Openness, dynamism, challenge, change and action. It's all about everyone taking responsibility and making things happen.'

The company sees Open Style as a kind of membrane that envelopes the three aspects of total business management – people, resources and systems (see Figure 11.9)

Everyone in an organisation both gives and receives a service. Roebuck takes the view that it is by looking for improvements in the way those services are supplied and received that the company will become more efficient and dynamic. The Open Style culture encourages Cow & Gate employees to view quality and service in the following light:

- Products and packaging and how well they work
- The information we give to our customers and our colleagues; its relevance, accuracy and speed
- The manner in which we deal with requests and give support
- The initiatives we take to improve processes and procedures

In order to improve both the services they give and the services they receive, Cow & Gate employees are encouraged to examine:

- What service is required (market research/find out/ask)?
- What service do we provide (as perceived by the receiver/ customer)?
- What can we change to improve the service (to the satisfaction of the receiver/customer)?
- What will it cost or save?
- How can it be actioned?

In essence, Cow & Gate sees Open Style as the creation of an environment whereby staff at all levels are encouraged and equipped to practise the 'Four A's':

Awareness

- to know what is happening (rather than nobody tells me)
- to find out what is happening (rather than prefer not to know)
- to care about what is happening (rather than none of my business)
- to analyse what is happening (rather than just accepting it)
- to develop/improve/add value to what is happening.

Attitude

- be positive (not defensive); an 'I will do' approach
- to seek change/improvement; (not wait to be told)
- develop solutions (not just present problems); make it happen
- take on challenge (rather than acquiesce)
- be challenging/confront problems (rather than opt for easy life); confrontation is constructive; confront issues not people
- discuss, explain and motivate (rather than dictate)
- be objective (rather than emotional)
- communicate openly (rather than guard knowledge for yourself)
- express your point of view (you cannot influence if you do not contribute).

Accountability

- be accountable
- take responsibility

Action

- make things happen.

In some cases Cow & Gate staff will need to take account of a fifth A – Authority. It will sometimes be necessary to seek the authority to undertake the improvement initiative.

Cascade

Initially, Roebuck tried to cascade the basic principles of the new culture through the organisation. He called a meeting of the top 20 senior managers to explain to them what he had in mind. The idea then was that each of them would become champions of the Open Style culture and would go away and explain the new approach to their staff so that it would filter down to the lower levels. Roebuck expected this to be a fairly protracted process taking perhaps two years, but what came as a big surprise to him was that he 'couldn't get it past square one. We couldn't actually get to the point where they didn't just acknowledge it, but believed in it to the extent they saw the need to change their own behaviours. It took us quite a long while to understand that.'

There was a real danger that the new approach would merely be seen as a managing director's fad and would eventually fade away. To avoid this, Roebuck decided to involve the senior managers in a programme of self-analysis. An industrial psychologist put the senior managers through some psychometric tests that allowed them to examine their own behaviours and attitudes. The hope was that they might see for themselves that they were standing in the way of bringing about change.

Roebuck brought the senior management team together again in December 1991 and informed them in no uncertain terms that he intended to push through the cultural change. He was totally authoritarian and uncompromising in expressing his determination to see the exercise through. There was no question of choice; they would embrace it or get left behind. He did, however, invite discussion and opinions about the best method of tackling it.

Some managers were still in favour of using the cascade method, rejecting the idea that they could not effectively handle the exercise in their own departments. However, a consensus view emerged that Roebuck should himself conduct identical presentations to groups of around 25 employees throughout the organisation. The advantage of this was that everyone would receive exactly the same message and those lower down the organisation would know that senior management had agreed to precisely the same approach as was being explained to them.

More than a dozen informal one-day gatherings were subsequently organised, at which Roebuck explained his idea of what Open Style management was all about. The participants were drawn from across the company and were of roughly equal status. Distribution clerks were mixed with secretaries and administrators from other departments, for example. This was to prevent staff feeling inhibited in the presence of senior managers. But there were other benefits from mixing employees in this way. Some of the participants found that even though they worked in the same building, they were only vaguely aware of what each other's job was.

Opportunities and Blockages

Syndicates were formed at the informal sessions to discuss, with the aid of an internal facilitator, participants' understanding of the new approach and to identify opportunities and possible blockages to achieving an Open Style culture. Typical blockages identified included:

- Managers block ideas and pay lip service to open style
- Insecure managers are worried by the possible bypass of their status and authority
- Not enough time
- Lack of confidence
- Ideas are hijacked by management.

Positive ideas and behaviours that were put forward to overcome the blockages included:

- Actions speak louder than words – let's just get on with it
- Lead by example
- Trust each other
- Be honest and say what you feel without fear of recrimination
- Train people to be more assertive and confident
- Communicate! – Traffic flows very quickly one way, but only ever gets to one end point!

- Give praise and credit where credit is due

As a result of these observations, general training and personal development programmes have been introduced covering such areas as performance coaching, assertiveness, organising meetings and counselling and self-appraisal techniques.

Secretaries' Forum

A number of unusual initiatives have grown out of the cross-fertilisation of ideas that was generated at the open style meetings. For example, all the secretaries at head office convened a meeting to examine common problems. They drew up a list of issues that they felt were impeding them in carrying out their work efficiently. But instead of leaving these as just whinges, they found solutions to most of the problems among themselves. A small number of problems that required higher authority were subsequently tackled by a secretaries' representative consulting directly with senior management.

One outcome has been that Cow & Gate no longer needs to employ temporary secretaries, since the resident secretaries have drawn up a schedule of secretaries' and managers' holidays to ensure that there will always be adequate coverage. This has resulted in cost savings and avoided work disruption.

In another example of personal initiative, Liz Mason, secretary to the head of personnel, has taken total responsibility for producing a company newspaper. The company had planned to produce a newspaper for some time, but nobody could find the time to tackle it. Liz took the initiative to form an editorial committee, gather the necessary information and supervise lay-out and printing. This is a classical example of taking initiative and filling a vacuum. The task was not delegated to Liz: she was aware of the need, adopted a positive 'I can do' attitude and got on and actioned it. This is precisely what the Open Style environment aims to encourage everyone to do in the business.

Liz's boss, Linda Chick, head of personnel, says: 'By all means retain your interest and coach and counsel and discuss progress, but if you make it too regimented the person undertaking the work loses ownership. To me, ownership is an important part of it, as well as the confidence that the individual is equipped with the skills and the resources to deliver the project.'

Another member of Cow & Gate's head office staff, Julie Freestone, sales support administrator, questioned the need for note pads with personal names on them. By producing general note pads that can be used by everyone, the company has saved a modest amount on printing costs, but more importantly has dramatically reduced the need for storage space.

Another example of Open Style success has been the responsibility and ownership that has been passed to the company's clinical nutrition sales force. In the past, the sales force had been set targets and objectives for their accounts by their managers, but Open Style has now reversed this process.

The sales executives approached management and asked to be involved in business development meetings where they gained first-hand experience of the division's strategic objectives. Armed with this knowledge, together with their own first-hand experience of their accounts, they now produce their own business plan for their territory and set their own targets and objectives. This plan is agreed with their line manager, but has resulted in each sales executive having ownership of his or her own realistic business objectives. The managers have also clearly benefited through gaining more time to further coach and develop their representatives and from the input of new ideas and expertise from their teams.

As the Open Style culture catches on at Cow & Gate, there is little doubt that personal initiatives of this nature will multiply and become a natural way of operating. The process is being encouraged by Open Style notice boards and by logging all the ideas in a special Open Style book. The time will undoubtedly come when everyone will take such actions for granted and it will be unnecessary to make a special feature of them. By then, taking responsibility for quality and service improvements will have become part and parcel of Cow & Gate's operating style.

Figure 11.10   'Three-legged stool' strategy

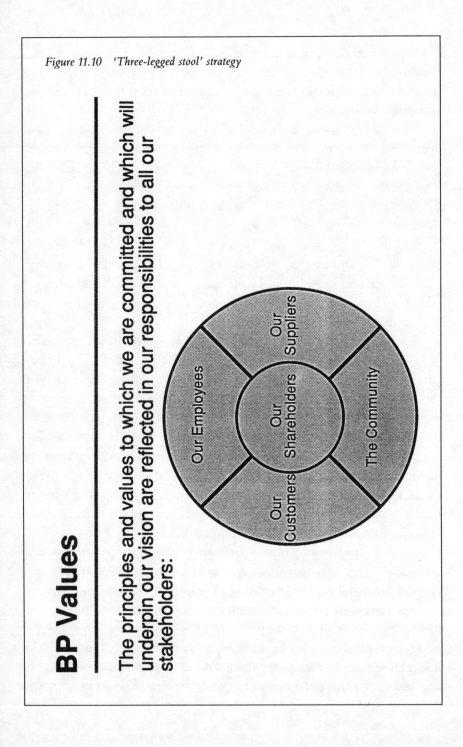

BP Values

The principles and values to which we are committed and which will underpin our vision are reflected in our responsibilities to all our stakeholders:

CASE STUDY – CULTURAL CHANGE AT BP

When Robert Horton was appointed chairman-elect of BP in 1989 he spent 12 months taking a fundamental look at how BP should gear itself for the decade ahead. Under the codename Project 1990, Horton set up a task force to examine to what extent the worldwide company needed to change if it was to remain competitive. It left no stone unturned in its comprehensive investigation of the best practices of the recognised 'benchmark' companies and its exploration of the opinions of the world's leading management thinkers. In addition, a huge survey of around 30 per cent of the 128,000 people employed by BP at that time was undertaken.

The end result of Project 1990 was a report that would lead to a fundamental re-shaping of BP and the way it operates.

BP decided that radical changes were needed in three principal areas – its corporate structure, which it felt was too complex; its work processes, particularly with regard to control, delegation and information sharing; and its culture. The oil company visualised its strategy in terms of a three-legged stool (see Figure 11.10). If one of the legs of the strategy were missing, the whole structure would collapse. For example, without a change of culture, the new approach to organisation structure and processes would fail to happen.

The proposals for change were thrashed out and agreed in December 1989 by the top 30 managers during a four-day meeting. 'The heart of the changes were about shifting the organisation from what you might call a command and control culture to one which was empowered,' explains Roy Williams, who initially advised BP as an independent consultant, but was later invited to join the company to help guide the change process.

The sweeping changes were set in motion as soon as Horton became chairman on 11 March 1990. Nobody was left in any doubt about the radical nature of the new approach. Some 12 layers of management in the previous organisation structure were reduced to six. Most of the 86 committees which had traditionally run the company and which acted as a centralised power-house, were

Figure 11.11   An Analysis of the Culture Change Decision at British Petroleum: Project 1990
Sara S. Grigsby, Harvard Business School 1992; Sartaj S. Alaj, Sloan School of Management 1992

Dimension	Type 1 (old style)	Type 2 (new style)
STRUCTURE		
Committees	86	6
# of business	11 or 12	4
Layers of management	12	6, Horton to first line supervisor
Corporate staff	2500 people	380 people
Organizational structure	matrix	divisional
Work unit	standing committee	temporary teams
Signatures for approval	12-13	2-3
Decision-making	top down	top down and bottom up
HUMAN RESOURCE MANAGEMENT		
Remuneration	high salaries	lower salary, + bonuses rewards
Performance evaluations	by tasks	by tasks and behaviours
CULTURE		
Communication	secrecy, information is power	information technology, teleconferencing, face to face, need to know
Information	held at top, as power and security	pushed down and shared surveys, bottom up
Risk taking	permission	creativity, trust
Errors	of omission	of commission
Diversity	British Lords	"Americanization"
People	title, grades, power, security	accountability, personal responsibility, empowerment
OTHER		
Environment	1970s: diversity into "energy"; many players 1980s: high margins consolidate and divest	1990: resources are finite, back to basics, a few big players
BP competitive strategy	financial and asset management	low cost, high tech develop core businesses
Name	British Petroleum	BP
Headquarters	high rise, closed offices, Britannic House	older Finsbury Circus, smaller, open plan
Titles	Chairman, Deputy Chairman	CEO, COO
Dividends	British model of twice/ year	American model of 4 times/year
Horton's salary	$2 million at Sohio	$800k as CEO

scrapped. The 2,500-strong corporate staff was reduced to around 400 people and later moved from the monolithic Moorgate tower building to the more compact Britannic House at Finsbury Circus. Where previously major items of capital expenditure required something of the order of a dozen signatures, two or three signatures suffice today. Under the old BP system, only managers at the highest levels in the company could authorise payments above $90 million. That was raised to $150 million overnight.

The full impact of BP's culture change was analysed by two US researchers, Sara S. Grigsby of Harvard Business School and Sartaj S. Alaj of the Sloan School of Management, who produced an unsolicited study of their findings (see Figure 11.11).

On the day Horton took over as chairman all 128,000 BP employees found a letter on their desks in their own language setting out the new vision and values that BP had committed itself to and the ways that these would be achieved.

Networks Instead of Committees

Two years down the line BP has made significant progress in achieving the changes it set out to make throughout its vast worldwide organisation, but it does not pretend to have found all the answers. For example, the large number of unwieldy committees at the centre are being replaced by networking. Networks tend to be a looser and much less formal system than committees and require a whole different cultural approach. Admits Williams: 'We are finding our way how to do it. We have learned some real lessons which say you must have a focal point. That's absolutely essential. You can't have a network out of focus.'

Williams himself is responsible for a management development and training network called the Learning Federation which spans the globe. He and four training managers from each of BP's main businesses provide the focal point of the network. They travel around the world co-ordinating policy with other parts of the network:

I visit Cleveland, for example, with one of the other members of the

Figure 11.12   BP Values

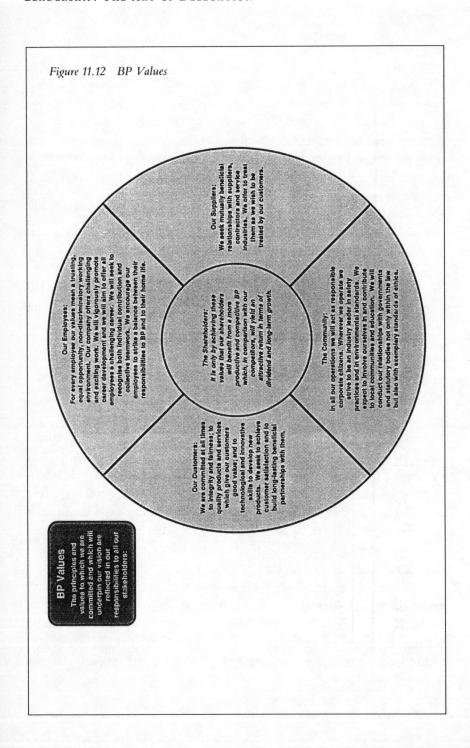

Figure 11.13   BP Values: Where we are now

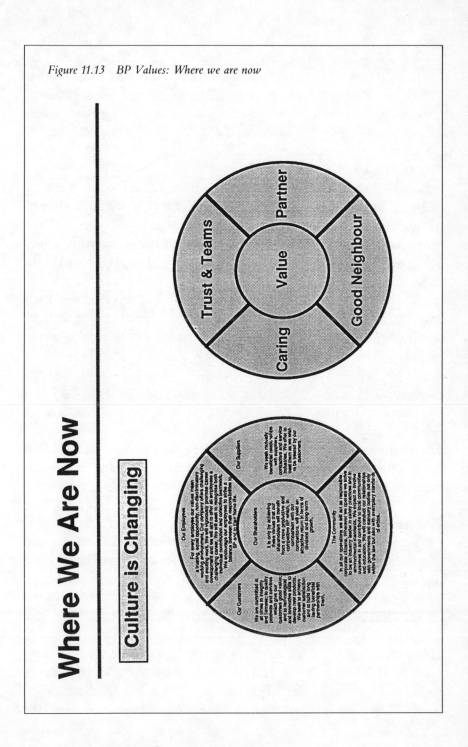

network and we link together with some 40 other people across the US.
We deal with problems that are relevant to the US in particular, but we
also tackle a topic which affects the whole organisation like performance
coaching. We then might move the issues on to Singapore, where
another member of the team would deal with it, like in a relay race.

The Courage to Change

It has taken a lot of courage for BP to pursue a course of such radical
change, but the company realised that in reality it had little choice.
As Williams points out: 'We really have to use the talents of the
people we've got to the fullest extent to gain the competitive edge.
The company realised that unless it made these changes it could be an
also-ran in the mid–to–late 1990s.'

Such a prospect was unthinkable and BP has replaced any such
pessimistic thoughts with a strategy based on excellence that declares
that it intends to be 'the world's most successful oil company in the
1990s and beyond'. To achieve that lofty goal it believes it needs to
satisfy five separate stakeholders – its shareholders, its employees, its
customers, its suppliers and the community in which it lives and
operates (see Figures 11.12 and 11.13). Williams says: 'We have to
satisfy all of them. If the only thing we tried to do was to get the
maximum return on capital for our shareholders, we could well find
we had lost our licence to operate in certain parts of the world, for
example.'

Top-down Cascade

To get across to its worldwide workforce how these values and
beliefs can be translated into operational reality, BP set in motion a
top-down cascade of information. It began with intense workshops
for the top 400 people in the company who in turn cascaded
information about the new approach throughout their sectors of the
company. The scale of this operation was quite breathtaking. BP
Oil, for example, which employs over 50,000 people, sent its top
team of 160 people to the initial workshops alongside colleagues
from other parts of the organisation. These 160 managers then
launched similar programmes in their own countries until the

information had filtered right through the organisation. In under eight months the cascade process went from BP Oil's chief executive to the people operating the filling stations in Vietnam, California and thousands of other locations around the world, telling them how it affected their job and how they fitted in to the total picture.

Task Forces

The Project 1990 study and subsequent BP-wide task forces identified several 'people areas' which the company needed to address. BP Chemicals formed a small team within its human resources division to tackle these challenges. As a means of empowering and involving its people to help that team, BP Chemicals set up an advisory task force drawn from the line. The task force was a diagonal slice of employees from a range of functions and locations around the world and from different levels in the organisation. The leader was one of the deputy chief executive officers and members came from the UK, United States, France and Switzerland. The task force gave all the elements of the programme a test run. It continually asked: Will this work? Is it user-friendly? Has anything been missed?

The task force now meets quarterly to discuss how implementation is going and opportunities for improvement.

After organising conferences and workshops for its top 350 employees, BP Exploration followed through with a series of self-initiated change workshops aimed at people in their own locations finding ways to implement the change and to seek improvements in performance. This was not a top-down process, but was initiated by local team leaders. It was coupled with facilitated 'fitness workshops' in many areas in which teams systematically concentrated on improving operating efficiency as a regular way of life.

Fundamental Shift of Behaviour

BP realised that if the changes were to become reality there needed to be a fundamental shift in managerial behaviour at BP. 'People have to behave in a way that is appropriate to the new culture and this gets right to the heart of what we mean by delegation,' explains Wiliams.

Figure 11.14 Where are we going? – BP's shift in attitude

Where are we going?

FROM		TO
Bureaucratic	→	Flexible, adaptable
Hierarchical	→	Team based
Dependent Culture	→	Self-confidence
Responsive	→	Pro-active
Paternalism	→	Partnership
Entitlement Culture	→	Rewarding skills, knowledge performance
Internal focus	→	External focus

BP is striving to bring about a major shift in attitudes (see Figure 11.14). For example, an entitlement culture has to give way to a culture that is based on rewarding skills, knowledge and performance. The traditional culture of BP was very benign – a job for life, a guaranteed career and above-average terms and conditions. 'In a sense you were part of a big club that looked after you for life – very paternalistic,' says Williams. 'That's absolutely for the birds in the 1990s. In restructuring and re-engineering the business people are having to leave; people are having to face up to radical changes.'

Rewarding skills, knowledge, performance and teamwork are at the heart of a new culture. 'For delegation to work, the reward structure has got to reflect what it is you want people to do in an empowered organisation,' argues Williams. 'In an empowered situation you are paid to operate inside and around the boundaries of your job. That's easy, but you also have to take responsibility for finding out such things as what others are doing and how your actions would impact on others before you make decisions outside the boundaries of your job and that's what you should be rewarded on.'

Open Behaviour

Exploring the kind of behaviours it needed to encourage in the new culture, BP arrived at the simple acronym of OPEN:

> **O**pen thinking
> **P**ersonal impact
> **E**mpowering
> **N**etworking

Essentially, BP believes it needs to help people to think differently about, and beyond, the boundaries of their routine jobs and to think less in a linear fashion. In addition, it believes, by and large, people at the top of the organisation need to reduce the amount of their personal impact and help the people further down the line to have more impact. Employees generally need to be encouraged to make comments and provide more feedback.

Williams stresses:

Empowering is an ongoing activity – upwards, downwards and sideways, because often you're empowering your boss or your peers as well as your subordinates. One of the errors in this area is to think of it solely as a downward process. People very often – particularly when they are under pressure – don't know what their staff will put up with. At a time of cutbacks, for example, empowering upwards is very important.

Williams also emphasises the importance of networking in making the whole process work: 'You can't have effective empowerment without effective networking. You might have tidy delegation but you won't have effective empowerment. In this organisation delegation is only a part of empowerment, not the other way around.'

Sense of direction

For empowerment and networking to thrive, BP knows it has to provide a sense of direction for all its operations around the world. Williams is fond of quoting a Ford senior executive who once said: 'I don't mind whether or not the cows are all pointing in the same direction as long as the herd is travelling West.' Adds Williams: 'You have got to provide an alignment when you delegate. You've got to know where the North Pole is. That's the first principle of delegation.'

To achieve this, each of BP's business operations has drawn up its own mission plan to link into the principles and values of the overall organisation. For example, BP Nutrition, a conglomerate of businesses ranging from slaughterhouses to pet food manufacturers and exotic prawn producers in Thailand, has established its own strategy within the broad framework of BP values. Each of the nine business streams within BP Nutrition has done the same. They don't all point precisely in the same direction, but the herd is travelling the same path.

The exercise took about eight months with employees at all levels of the business participating. It culminated with about 200 people from BP Nutrition closeting themselves in an Antwerp Hotel for three days, drafting and re-drafting the strategies needed to drive the process forward. A lot of horse-trading went on, according to Williams, since the various strategies had to live within overall budgetary limits.

Observes Williams:

The point I want to stress is that to get the delegation process right, you have to have coherence at the strategic level. Whether we are talking about a big company like BP or one of the smaller businesses, unless the bits are fitting into some shape, people can't be properly delegated to other than by instruction. The more you move towards empowerment, the more you have to invest in the infrastructure. You can't do it by just saying: 'go and be empowered'. You've got to put the systems and support in place. So there's been a systematic process in BP of cascading down the overall aims, ambitions and strategies against a set of explicit values.

At the end of the process Mary in Scunthorpe or Jean in Provence should understand exactly what is expected of them, where they fit into the overall picture and what the bounds of their authority are; what behaviours and initiatives are likely to be rewarded. Inevitably, the message has got through more successfully to some parts of the organisation than others. In some areas it has gone almost unbelievably according to the script; in others there have been problems and pockets of resistance. But in general Williams is more than satisfied with progress:

We are only two years into what we see as a six to seven year process and we have systematically tried to change the process of delegation and tried to empower people. It is no longer controlled from the centre. Each part of the organisation must find its own way of doing it provided they come within the general framework. The common values are what we call the corporate glue.

The resignation of Robert Horton in June 1992 has raised some questions about whether the impetus will be sustained. All the indications are, however, that the change process is now unstoppable and that the new culture has become embedded in the way BP does business. Time will tell whether this proves to be the case.

EXAMPLES OF EMPOWERMENT AT BP

BP believes that empowerment offers each of its employees the opportunity to contribute directly. Success, it maintains, is measured by the accumulation of a host of local achievements realised on a continuing basis rather than high-profile one-off improvements. Here are a few examples:

Decentralisation at BP Greece
BP Greece has traditionally suffered from a 'public service' mentality which finds wider expression in the country as a whole. Many staff felt management either lacked the will or the ability to change it. A working team of middle managers was charged therefore with identifying the changes they would like to see to improve motivation and profit-orientation. Two of them conducted in-depth interviews with management and staff and came up with a number of organisational and development changes designed to remove bureaucracy, decentralise decision-making and create a climate which encouraged success.

Both culturally and organisationally, managers at BP Greece were accustomed to a highly centralised style of management, where most business decisions were referred to the general manager. Since this was undesirable both from the point of view of managerial effectiveness and motivation, the challenge was to decentralise and delegate decision-making to business managers, whilst providing the necessary transitory support.

The first step was to encourage resolution of issues between managers before having to bring them to management meetings for decision. The next step was to cut back the number of formal management meetings. The process has been more rapid than management had expected. They now mostly resolve problems amongst themselves and few issues are referred to the general manager for decision as opposed to information. Apart from a quarterly 'communication' forum, formal meetings have been replaced by *ad hoc* sessions at the request of one of the managers after discussion with his peers. The effect on management motivation has been quite marked.

Britannic House IT Project

The Britannic House IT project involves major capital expenditure in a complex project to replace existing IT systems and encourage information sharing amongst corporate centre teams at Finsbury Circus. The managing director responsible appointed a project director to manage the project, but did not impose the traditional impediments of a project board, management committees, steering groups or rigid upward reporting. The project is being delivered on time and within budget – a rarity for IT projects. The approach was: 'Here's what you have to do, here's the money – go and do it.'

Personal Behaviour Change

A senior member of BP's regional centre staff has made a concerted effort to modify his style of dealing with employees. This has included spending time reviewing progress, establishing requirements, soliciting concerns, and in general being more caring. This change was initially met with suspicion and cynicism. Over time a mutual trust that the change is real has developed. A more productive work environment has resulted.

Office Design in Australia

In designing its new head office, BP Australia actively sought the maximum input from staff. Four questionnaires were sent to all head office staff exploring attitudes to location, facilities and services. There was a high response rate. In addition, ten user groups were established, each with a representative cross-section of staff. These covered IT, conferencing, training, communications, dining, HSE, facilities and art. BP Australia is convinced that the exercise has increased employee motivation and that 'ownership' of the new building is high, leading to greater morale and productivity.

Combined Team for Automotive Products

BP Chemicals had identified a number of options for the automotive market. Similarly, BP Oil, starting from the position of wishing to attract customers to its forecourt shops, was keen to expand and improve its automotive product sales through its distribution and marketing channels.

To develop the opportunities, people from BP Chemicals and BP Oil have joined forces informally to form a team, along with colleagues from BP Research involved in product development and qualification testing. This is an initiative from relatively junior levels in the organisation, which, among other things, has avoided the risk of senior management spending time in discussion about who would get what share of the costs and benefits when the new products were launched.

Instead the focus has been on identifying new market opportunities, bringing together people with first-hand knowledge from wherever they are located in BP and getting the products to market by the fastest route. Senior management's role has been to encourage and coach and to facilitate by removing constraints.

Oil Field Cost Control

A new approach to controlling costs and reducing losses has been implemented at BP's Welton oil field in the UK. Field personnel are being empowered to control, monitor and understand spending patterns.

The operation supervisory level below the budget responsibility officer was given the previous year's spending figures and a review was conducted, broken down by site and then by well. This exposed the high cost items and more specifically which wells were responsible. The high cost area information was shared with well operators and ideas for alternative methods and practices were discussed.

Implementation of these ideas had an immediate impact in many areas. Repair and maintenance costs, for example, were reduced by 33 per cent by using existing BP equipment and resources while eliminating contract hire. The review found that this was the first time most field staff had been exposed to itemised spending.

Bibliography

Barham, K., and Rassam, C. (1989) *Shaping the Corporate Future*, London: Unwin Hyman

Bennis, W. (1989) *On Becoming a Leader*, London: Century Business

Bennis, W. (1989) *Why Leaders Can't Lead*, San Francisco and London: Jossey Bass

Blanchard, K., Zigarmi, P. and Zigarmi, D., *Leadership and the One Minute Manager*, London: Fontana

Peters, T., and Waterman, R.H. (1982) *In Search of Excellence*, New York and London: Harper & Row

Smythe, J., Dorward, C., and Reback, J. (1992) *Corporate Reputation*, London: Century Business

Toffler, A. (1970) *Future Shock*, London: Bodley Head

Index

accountability, 1–2, 19, 23, 213
adhocracy, 31, 150
Alaj, Sartaj S, 220, 221
anarchy, 53
Ashridge Management College, 14, 15, 34, 73, 100, 158
Ashridge Management Research Group, 47, 49
Ashridge leadership programme, 50
Assessment Design Services, 34, 58, 95, 98, 102, 109, 119
attitude, 213
authority,
   concept of, 1–2, 19
   reduction in acceptance of, 52–3
   subordinates, of, 92–3, 213
awareness, 212

BAA, 99
BOC, 42–3
BP, 32, 33, 34, 42, 108, 219–32
   Britannic House IT Project, 221, 231
   Learning Federation, 221
   Project 1990, 219–10, 225
   Welton oil field, 232
BP Australia, 231
BP Chemicals, 232

BP Exploration, 225
BP Greece, 230
BP Nutrition, 228
BP Oil, 224, 225, 232
BP Research, 232
Barham, Kevin, 99
benchmarks, 172–3
Benefits Agency, the, 29–30
Bennis, Warren, 31, 53–5, 57–8, 148, 149
Blanchard, Kenneth, H., 120–2, 164
blockages, 215
Boots the Chemists, 68
Booz Allen & Hamilton, 47–8
British Airways, 62
British Telecom, 32, 38–9, 108
Brown, Dr Barry, 14, 15, 47, 48, 75, 78, 88
Bruce, Alex, 100–102
Buse, Rodney, 199–206
Butler, Sir Robin, 29, 30

cascade, 214–5, 224
Central Middlesex Trust Hospital, 30
Chick, Linda, 135–6, 216
Citizen's Charter, 29, 38
Civil Service, 29

command organisations,
   fallacies of, 85
   generally, 69–70, 76
communication, 168, 193
company advisory board (COAB),
   153–7
confidence, 9, 25
continuous improvement, 69,
   210–13
control,
   concept of, 14–15
   cost, 232
   external, 79–83
   informal, 45
   internal, 79–83
Coopers Deloitte, 64, 74–5
core competencies, 193
Corporate Reputation, 46
Cow & Gate, 135, 206–18
culture,
   change, 219–21
   open style. *See* management,
      open.
customer satisfaction, 160
Curnow, Barry, 24, 25

decentralisation, 48–51, 230
de-layered organisations, 2, 15, 31–6
Dennison, Stuart, 38
de-skilling, 74–5
delegation,
   benefits, 26–7
   by degrees, 119
   definition, 14
   crisis, 99–100
   criteria,
      what not to, 89–90
      what to, 88–9
      who to, 90–1, 118–132
   emergency, 100–102
   fallacies, 26
   financial decisions, 102
   founder-managers, 143–147

insufficient, 11–15
   goals, 88
   legal work, 103–6
   limits, 137–9
   planning, 23
   problems of, 98–9
   process, 88–107
   reluctance, 5, 16–18
   resistance, 25
   rewards, 9–10, 20
   teams, 148–171
   technical decisions, 102
   tips, 106
   triggers, 22
   upward, 136–140. 204
   whizz kids, to, 129–132
demotivation, 73
Digital Equipment Co, 32, 33,
   39–41, 66, 72, 152, 165–9
Director, 46
Dixon, Bob, 6, 16, 17, 19, 21
Document Company, The, 173
Donaldson, Liz, 37
Dow, 162
Drucker, Peter, 34
Durcan, Jim, 14, 16, 18, 19, 34, 43,
   44, 49–62, 61, 65–6, 70, 73,
   76–81, 83, 100, 102
Durcan's control grid, 79–81

EETPU, 153
Edge, The, 103
Egan, Sir John, 99
empowered organisations, 69, 76,
   83
empowerment,
   BP, in, 230
   Britain, in, 84
   criticisms of, 64–6
   definition, 57
   examples, 67, 78
   generally, 2, 57–86
   guidelines, 77

Rank Xerox, in, 169-191,
   teams, 149
Esso Petroleum, 68

feedback, 133-142
   immediate, 134
   negative, 133
   upward, 136-140
   varied, 134
Field, Sir Malcolm, 205
Financial Times, The, 33, 42
Fine, Alan, 162
Flexiplace scheme, 38
Ford, 228
founder-managers, 143-147
Fowler, Alan, 66-7
funnel of specialisation, 17
Future Shock, 149

Garnett, John, 151
Giordiano, Dick, 42-3
globalisation, 46-8, 50, 51
Grigsby, Sara S, 220-221
Guy, Richard, 158

Haffenden, Mike, 192-3, 195, 197
Handy, Charles, 59
Hanson, 18
Harley Davidson, 73
Harris, George, 155
Harris, John, 47-8
Hartlepool Power Station, 62
Harvard Business School, 150,
   220-1
Hazlewood, Gerry, 145-7
Hedges, Pat, 46
Heinz, 207
Henley Centre for Forecasting, 37
Henley Management College, 14,
   17, 22-3, 28, 41, 61, 64, 80, 108,
   119, 122-3, 141, 149
Henry Ford Hospital, 78
Hersey, Paul, 120-22, 164

Herzberg, Frederick, 6, 68
Hewlett-Packard, 191-8
high performers, 126
Hill, Roy, 38
Hillier, Jenny, 30
hoshin, 171, 191, 194-5
Horton, Robert, 33, 42, 219, 221,
   229

IBM, 162
ICI, 151
In Search of Excellence, 32
Independent, The, 37-8, 42
Independent Assessment and
   Research Centre, The, 14, 47,
   75, 88
Industrial Society, The, 6, 16, 19,
   21, 88-9, 151
initiatives, 63, 209
Insideout Company, 162
instability, 59
Institute of Personnel Management,
   24
intelligence, 126-7
International Management, 45
Ivey, Nick, 106

Jaguar, 99-100
James, Allan, 194-5, 198
job enrichment, 3, 149
job satisfaction, 6, 26
job security, loss of, 52
Jones, Les, 171, 180, 184-5

Kinsley Lord, 60, 62-3, 69, 76-7,
   83-6, 150
Knight, Tony, 14, 16, 61, 64, 119,
   122, 141-2

leadership, 7, 15, 54-5, 199
   situational, 120-122
   teams, of, 151-62
   through quality, 175

vacuum, 53
leadership through quality, 175
Lever, Chris, 165-9
Lloyds of London, 158
London Borough of Enfield, 38
London Business School, 42
Lorenz, Christopher, 33, 42

Major, John, 29
management,
    behaviour, 225-8, 231
    by objectives, 66-7
    definition, 1
    general, 8
    open, 46, 135, 210-18, 227
    senior, 16
    style, 182
    training, 8, 22, 108-9
Marchant, David, 202-4
Mason, Liz, 216
Masters, David, 105
McGregor, 82
McLaren, Fiona, 103-5
Mills, Quinn, 62, 150
motivation, 6

NASA, 78
National Economic Development
    Office, 37
National Health Service, 28, 62, 78
Nestle, 55
networking, 41-6, 221
Nuclear Electric, 62, 68
Nutricia, 207-8
On Becoming a Leader, 54
opportunities, 215
organisations,
    command, 69-70, 76, 85
    de-layered. 2, 15, 31-6
    empowered, 69-70, 76, 83
    future development of, 55-6
    Japanese, 59-62
Our Price Music, 201-2

Oxfordshire County Council, 38

PA Management Consultants, 66,
    74
Pantling, Shaun, 169-171
Parcel Force, 46
parent and child, 73
performance,
    coaching, 3, 108-116
    management system, 66-7
perfection, desire for, 25
Personnel Management, 37, 41, 55-7
Peters, Tom, 28, 32, 70-71, 73, 158
persuasion, 24
policy deployment, 174
Post Office, 32
potential, 10
praise, 135
Prentice, Graham, 55-6
productivity gains, 62
promotion, 7, 21
pyramid,
    inverted, 179. See also
        organisations, de-layered.

quality,
    leadership through, 175

Rainmaking, 103, 105
Rassam, Clive, 99
Ransomes, 145
Rothwell, Sheila, 17, 20-3, 41, 65,
    80, 123, 149
Rank Organisation, The, 173
Rank Toshiba, 152
Rank Xerox (UK) Ltd,
    generally, 32, 152, 169-91
    future development, 184
recruitment, 204
responsibility,
    devolved, 28-29
    nature of, 1
    table of, 200-201

Richard, Michael, 29
Roebuck, Peter, 206–15
Rolls Royce, 7, 118
Royal Liverpool Children's
    Hospital, 68–9

satisfiers, 6
Savage, Adrian, 34–6, 45, 48, 58–9,
    98–9, 102, 109, 113–5, 119–20,
    126–8, 135
Scott, Phil, 39–40
secretaries, 22, 216
self-development, 195–6
shadow organisations, 45
Shaping the Corporate Future, 99
Shell, 162
Sherwood Computer Services, 35,
    151, 157–64
single status, 153
situational leadership, 120–22
Sloan School of Management,
    220–1
Smythe Dorward Lambert, 46
Smythe, John, 46
specialisation, 17
Speechly Bircham, 103–6
Stanton, Michael, 74
Stanworth, Celia, 37
Stanworth, Professor John, 37
status, 164
subordinates,
    authority, 92–3
    confidence in, 9, 13
    delegation to, 91–8
    development, 88, 108–16
    energies, 76
    potential of, 10
    progress, 94
    inspiration of, 10
    responsibility, 24–5, 94
    talents, 70
    training, 92
Stockton Lecture, 42

Taffinder, Dr Paul, 64, 75
talents,
    tapping of, 70
Tartan offshore oil platform, 100
taskforces, 225
Taylor, Frederick, 33, 199, 203
Taylor, Professor Bernard, 23–4,
    28–31, 64, 108
Taylor, Stephen, 60, 62–3, 69, 150
teamwork, 6, 152
teams, 148–71
    client, 158–64
    leadership, 151, 160
    self-managed, 167–71
teleworking, 37–41
Texaco, 100–102
Theory Y, 82
Thomas, Bob, 157–64
Thomas, Michael, 66, 74
Thomson, Des, 157
Thorn EMI, 118
time constraints, 25
Toffler, Alvin, 149
Tombs, Lord, 7, 118
Toshiba Consumer Products, 152–7
Toyota, 59–60
training, 92

Unigate, 207
Unilever, 206
University of Cincinnati, 54
Volvo, 149, 169
volunteers,
    identification of, 75

W.H. Smith, 198–206
W.H. Smith Group, 201, 205
W.H. Smith Retail, 201–2
Waterstones, 201
Westwood Engineering, 145–7
whizz kids, 129–132
Why Leaders Can't Lead, 57
Wilkins, Sir Graham, 118

Williams, George, 153
Williams, Roy, 219, 221, 224–9
work groups, 167–171
Wright, Alistair, 32–3, 66, 72
Wylfa Power Station, 68

Xerox Corporation of America, 173

Zelmer, Vernon, 170, 173, 175, 177, 179–84